PRAISE FOR L.A. WRITE[
90-DAY REWRITE WOR

"The 90-Day Rewrite Workshop taught me how to infuse the first draft of my novel with the kind of left-brain logic that is required if one's story is to have a strong narrative arc without sacrificing the right-brain passion which went into writing the first draft. The workshop kept the focus right where it needed to be, on the nature of the relationship between my characters and on the dilemma(s) that my novel needed to resolve. The workshop taught me how to re-embrace my novel in a way that made the tasks of revising as pleasurable and productive as the white-heat intensity that went into writing the first draft. Al teaches you to live in your scenes and set aside the hypercritical surveillance that can plague the rewrite process. I did more work in less time, and with greater satisfaction in this workshop than ever before."

—FRANK B. WILDERSON, III
(author of *Incognegro: A Memoir of Exile and Apartheid,*
winner of the American Book Award and the
National Endowment of the Arts Literature Fellowship)

"The 90-Day Rewrite gave me all the tools I needed to refine my first draft and get closer to the heart of my story. Al's highly effective techniques stay with you as a writer and give you the confidence to finish your work and prepare it for publication."

—JENNIFER SCOTT
(author of *Lessons from Madame Chic: Twenty Stylish Secrets
I Learned While Living in Paris,* Simon and Schuster)

"The workshop provides writers at every level with a safe place to engage their creativity. Through a combination of in-class writing, queries into structure, and repeated one-on-one dialogues, writers gain access to the subconscious, where the emotional truth of the story abides. The classes are intense. Al gives his all, while allowing writers to discover for themselves the strongest possible path to a completed work. I couldn't be more grateful."

—KAREN PALMER
(author of *Border Dogs* and *All Saints*)

"Countless books, courses, and websites promise to take your writing to the next level, but fail to go much beyond the basics. The 90-Day Rewrite process actually comes through on the promise by encouraging – forcing – the writer to dig ever deeper in order to discover psychological depth and complexity. Highly recommended for those who really do want to move beyond mere plot mechanics."

—JANICE MACDONALD
(author of Harlequin's *Practice Makes Perfect*)

"The 90-Day Rewrite has given me the tools to become a stronger storyteller as well as teaching me to write from the heart and not from the head, and teaching me to be actively curious about my characters and the world in which they live."

—ROMA MAFFIA
(author/actress *Nip/Tuck*)

the 90-day rewrite

by
Alan Watt

A publication of The 90-Day Novel Press

Library of Congress PCN 2012935179

ISBN 978-0-9831412-1-1

JOIN L.A. WRITERS' LAB

Free membership includes:

- Special member's only discounts on a variety of products and services.
- Free tele-conference workshops with Al Watt and others.
- Live tele-conference interviews and Q&A's with established authors and screenwriters on craft, career and navigating life as a professional writer.
- A monthly newsletter with writing tips, author interviews, and info on upcoming workshops.

Q: How do I become a member?

A: Go to lawriterslab.com. Join the mailing list. Congratulations, you are now a member!

DEDICATION

To the students and teachers at L.A. Writers' Lab.
And to Mary-Beth – I would not change a thing.

TABLE OF CONTENTS

PART ONE
PREPARATION

PART TWO
THE 90-DAY REWRITE:
THE PROCESS OF REVISION

PART THREE
I'M DONE. NOW WHAT?

INTRODUCTION

"Education is not the filling of a pail, but the lighting of a fire."   —WILLIAM BUTLER YEATS

Is it possible to rewrite a book in 90 days? Yes, it is. I have done it, and so have many other writers. The goal of this book, however, is not to insist upon such a task, but to provide a framework that puts an end to procrastination and perfectionism and guides you through a second pass of your novel or work of creative nonfiction.

L.A. Writers' Lab was formed in March 2002 to help writers get the stories from their imaginations to the page. Over the past ten years, the material in this book has been developed at the lab through practical instruction and consistent feedback to help writers who were getting bogged down by the myriad vagaries of the rewrite process. By setting goals and having clearly defined guideposts this process has helped many writers complete their work in a timely manner.

As the rewrite process involves moving between the left and right brain, this workbook is structured to approximate that experience. The first section, *Preparation*, contains an overview of the process and an in-depth discussion of story structure. It is followed by a series of left-brain *Technical Matters*. The second section is the *90-Day Rewrite* workshop, which is divided into thirteen weeks, with each week addressing a key stage in the hero's journey. The weekly summaries provide an overview of the work to be covered that week, while the daily letters are focused on various aspects of the process and offer a single daily directive.

The third section discusses what to do with your manuscript once you have completed your rewrite.

There is an apocryphal tale of members of the Glenn Miller Band who were traveling to a gig when their bus broke down in a blizzard. To get to the show they had to trudge for six hours through the snow. While walking past a farmhouse where a family sat together, warm and dry, eating their Thanksgiving dinner, the tuba player, stumbling under the weight of his instrument turned to the sax man and said, "Look at those poor bastards. What kind of life is that?"

The writer's life is filled with endless unknowns and terminable dreads, but when we acknowledge that the thrill of creation is its own reward, we are the lucky ones.

—AL WATT
Los Angeles

AN OVERVIEW OF THE PROCESS

The goal of the 90-Day Rewrite is simple, but not easy. We want our story to live. It is helpful to have a basic confidence in the arc of our hero's journey before getting more specific with character, dialogue, and the refining of prose. We are seeking to create a story that amuses and entertains while capturing the complexity and truth of the human experience. This can be daunting as there is often a degree of rigidity in our relationship to our first draft. We may fear that if it is not told precisely as we had imagined it, it will not work, and yet our current draft may feel somewhat unsatisfying. The biggest challenge of the rewrite is in making a thousand little changes while honoring the integrity of our initial premise. In other words, how do we keep the patient alive during surgery? By stepping back and getting the lay of the land, we can approach our rewrite with a clear sense of our objectives.

READING OUR FIRST DRAFT

Our first task is to read our manuscript. We do not judge it. If we want to make notes, we keep them simple. It can be surprising to discover that we love parts we thought were monotonous, and are bored stiff by sections we thought profound. There may even be whole sections we have no recollection of having written. Sometimes, in our creative frenzy, we were not even conscious of what we were writing.

DILEMMA

As the rewrite process involves a gradual movement from the general to the specific, we must first identify the dilemma at the heart of our story, as this will provide us with a sense of what our story is really about. By getting underneath the plot and identifying the primal forces within, we'll develop a deeper understanding of why we wrote what we wrote in our first draft, and will have a greater confidence in the editing required to fully realize our work. Prior to beginning the 90-Day Rewrite, the section on dilemma will offer some insight into exploring our story's theme.

TECHNICAL MATTERS

The Technical Matters section is the final stage before beginning our 90-Day Rewrite. It provides a series of tools, techniques and examples to illustrate the mechanics of storytelling and prose. While these are the paints and the brushes, our manuscript is the canvas. The purpose of this section is to arm ourselves with the basic tools to make our story more alive. Our characters and prose are in service to our theme. Technique without imagination is worthless, and imagination without technique will cloud our work's intended meaning.

A NEW OUTLINE

In Week One we are going to create a new outline. Our story is actually quite malleable. With a deeper understanding of the dilemma at the heart of our story, and by staying connected to the nature of what we are attempting to express, we become open to the possibility of reordering events, conflating characters and scenes, layering material from other scenes, and exploring creative ways to dramatize exposition. In doing so, our story moves in the direction of its most fully realized form.

We now know so much more about our characters and story than we did during our first draft. This outline is not simply a re-hashing of the events from the first draft of our novel. Rather, we are using our first draft as a point of departure, while taking into account the variety of scenes we feel may no longer be required in the next draft, or the scenes that still need to be written, events reordered, information relayed in a more dramatic or clearer way, character inconsistencies clarified, redundancies banished, and so on. All of these factors are taken into account as we write a new out-line with a clearer sense of the story. We take our time, granting our imagination the authority in considering the most effective way to tell our story. By inquiring into the structure questions at the back of the book, we are aided in completing our outline.

STORY STRUCTURE

We are not interested in the three-act structure as a formulaic ap-proach to story that reduces human behavior to simplistic cliché, but rather as a way to deepen our understanding of our story so that we can recognize the underlying meaning of what our subconscious did naturally.

We never want to force our story into our *idea* of how it should be structured. Our original impulse was valid. We can trust it and return to it over and over again, even as the story continues to be reshaped. We may have a better sense of story structure than we think we do. It seems the art of storytelling involves a willingness to surrender our idea of the way the story should be told, for the way it actually wants to be told. In the rewrite, we are attempting to marry the wildness of our first draft with a more specific sense of struc-ture. Our writing can support all that our imaginations can conjure when we distill our ideas to their nature. As we notice patterns and make connections at the level of plot, character and theme, we are more likely to make changes to the work without veering off the narrative throughline.

THE 90-DAY REWRITE:
THE PROCESS OF REVISION

Using what we have learned in the Preparation section, and having created a new outline, we begin rewriting our manuscript in Week Two. As we are rewriting our story in a modular fashion, we will rewrite roughly three or four pages a day, and each week will address a new story point in the hero's journey. We are going to spend three weeks rewriting Act One, six weeks on Act Two, and the final three weeks on Act Three. Each section begins with a summary outlining the work to be covered that week, followed by an overview of story questions to be considered. By dividing our work into sections, we give ourselves weekly goals to reach.

As this is not a linear process, we may notice that some of the changes we make are affecting other areas of our manuscript. It makes sense to address these areas while they are fresh in our minds. By making the necessary changes, we can return to the apportioned section for that week with a clearer sense of our story. As one change begets the next, our work gradually moves toward its most fully realized version.

THE 90 DAILY LETTERS

The daily letters address specific process issues. Although they cover a broad range of topics, they are also meant to address the area being covered that week.

At the bottom of each letter is a TODAY section offering a daily directive. These directives are suggestions designed to deepen our relationship to our work. **The directives are not meant to be the only work that we do that day.** The rewrite process involves performing a series of tasks in concert, many of which are covered in the technical matters section. As we work through roughly three or four pages each day, beginning in Week Two, we are performing a variety of tasks such as writing new material, editing, reordering material, fine-tuning our prose, tweaking our dialogue, and clarifying our theme.

PITFALLS OF THE REWRITE

The challenge is to know what to expel and what to keep. How often have we given our work to a friend for notes only to receive opinions? "I like this scene, but not that one." It is unusual to find someone who reads our work with genuine curiosity as to how our plot supports our theme. The consequence of getting opinion-based notes is that it can lead the writer to lose connection to his work. When we show our work too soon, we are abdicating authority over it. Certainly there comes a point where we need a fresh eye, but until we have done all we can do, we jeopardize our relationship to our initial impulse.

There are all sorts of ways to go off track in our attempt to "improve" our first draft, and they can be boiled down to one word: fear.

1. Fear that it will be misunderstood, and so we simplify the conflict, killing the aliveness of our characters' motivations.

2. Fear that it will never be good. We become impatient and rush because we are not really sure anything will come of it. It is inevitable that at some point in the rewrite we will grow tired of our work. This is an occupational hazard. Familiarity breeds contempt, and we are going to become very familiar with our words.

3. Fear we are doing it wrong. We may become convinced that our process is invalid, or confused about what to keep, what to remove, and where to go from here.

4. Fear that we are wasting our time. This is similar to the fear that it won't be good, but it includes the larger fear

that nothing we do will ever be good. This fear can spread until it has us where it wants us—paralyzed, and awash in self-doubt.

The antidote to fear is to continually, one day at a time, stay out of the result and place ourselves squarely in the process.

A FINAL WORD ON PROCESS

This book is intended to provide guidance, insight and encouragement, but is not intended to be the final word. A book on creativity that insists upon one right way misses the point. When the thrill of creation is its own reward, we are more inclined to create something lasting and meaningful. When we write with the sole intention of getting published, we squander our gifts. Sure, we want our work to be read by others, but the paradox is that unless we connect to our uniqueness, we have little to offer. My goal is to help you develop a process that makes your work as compelling and dynamic as possible. If you firmly disagree with anything in this book, trust your instincts, and write what you know to be true. You are the authority over your work.

Let's begin our preparation.

PART ONE

preparation

DILEMMA:
THE SOURCE OF OUR STORY

A t the heart of every story lies a dilemma. It is not a question of whether or not our protagonist has a dilemma, but rather how effectively it has been explored. By exploring our protagonist's dilemma, we are led to the most dynamic version of our story. In fact, the dilemma is the source of our story, and it is from this place that all tension and conflict arises. Exploring the dilemma helps distill our prose to its clearest meaning. It sheds light on what does not belong, those random digressions that are not germane to the central conflict and that may obfuscate its meaning. It offers clues to what still needs to be rewritten and leads us to the most effective order of events.

STORY MAXIM #1: The purpose of story is to reveal a transformation.

By definition, a dilemma cannot be figured out. In order to connect to it, we must become invested in our characters. Sometimes there can be a tendency to hold so tightly to our idea of our characters that we choke them into submission, and are left with two-dimensional versions of what they could have been. By inquiring into the dilemma, we are free to explore our characters in surprising ways, and our story can move inexorably to a climax that reveals a transformation.

WHAT IS A DILEMMA?

A dilemma is a problem that cannot be solved without creating another problem. Many writing books talk about the dramatic problem, the *thing* that the protagonist is attempting to solve or overcome through the story. However, after years of working with writers, I have discovered that the notion of a dramatic problem actually limits the writer's understanding of his story. When we approach our story as if our protagonist is struggling with a problem, we tend to try to figure out a way to fix it, which can short-circuit our work, because underlying our protagonist's "apparent" problem is a dilemma. By inquiring into the dilemma, we begin to see our story from a wider perspective.

STORY MAXIM #2: Problems are *solved*, while dilemmas are *resolved* through a shift in perception.

It is unlikely that many writers are even conscious of their story's dilemma. In fact, I have talked to many successful writers who only seem to have a vague sense of it. They are aware of the mechanics – that each scene must contain tension, and that this tension should build through the story to its eventual climax. However, this alone is not always enough to create a story that feels thoroughly satisfying – even for the author. There can be that nagging feeling that something has been left unsaid, yet they are not able to articulate it. There is often great value in becoming clear on the dilemma because it can expose aspects of our characters that lead to more dynamic situations in our work.

PLOT VERSUS THEME

The problems that our protagonist encounters address our story's plot, but when we explore these problems as a whole we begin to notice underlying patterns that reveal the dilemma, and this relates to our theme. Typically, we tend to see our situations as problems. We may believe that if only we got the promotion our life would be better, or that if we lost weight, or quit smoking, or got a girlfriend, or moved out of our parent's basement, then everything would be just fine. However, underlying these apparent problems lie a deeper reason for why we have not accomplished our goal. The fact is that the meaning we attach to our desire actually prevents us from achieving our goal. It is not that our desire is bad or wrong, it is that the meaning we attach to it assures its lack of success.

WHERE DID OUR STORY COME FROM?

Perhaps our story began as a premise, a character, or a single idea, but underlying these impulses was a subconscious quest for resolution. The creative impulse seeks to make order from chaos, to contextualize a series of events with the intention of making new meaning from them. As storytellers, we are drawn to unresolved situations: Will Jimmy Stewart leave Bedford Falls? Will Dorothy's dreams come true somewhere over the rainbow? Will Harry Potter triumph over Lord Voldemort?

These questions appear to present a problem but they are actually providing a context through which we can explore a resolution to a dilemma. If Jimmy Stewart did leave Bedford Falls at the end of *It's a Wonderful Life*, we would be disappointed because he would not have wrestled with his dilemma and learned that his life is already wonderful. Similarly, if Dorothy's dreams did come true somewhere over the rainbow, we would miss the point, and if Harry Potter simply destroyed Lord Voldemort and that was the end of it, there would be no context for the theme—which is that good and evil must coexist.

STORY MAXIM #3: The desire to write is connected to the desire to resolve something we seek to understand. By noticing the central dilemma in our story, we will see where it exists in our life. By exploring its resolution in our life, we will find its resolution in our story.

Here are some examples of dilemmas:
- I want intimacy, but I do not want to reveal myself.
- I want to be successful, but I do not want to overshadow my father.
- I want to move on from my mother's death, but I do not want to say goodbye to her.
- I want to know what happens when I die, so that I will know how to live.
- I want to have faith, but I do not trust God.
- I want to be forgiven, but I do not want to confess.
- I want love, but I don't want to commit.
- I want to control my thoughts, so that I can have peace.
- I want to be true to myself, but I do not want to disappoint anybody.

Notice how dilemmas are visceral. They engage the imagination and demand an emotional experience.

HOW DO WE IDENTIFY THE DILEMMA IN OUR STORY?
There are two ingredients to a dilemma:
1. A powerful desire.
2. A false belief.

DESIRE: OUR PROTAGONIST'S GOAL
If we believe that love will make us complete, we might set out on a search for love and misinterpret each relationship that does not resemble completeness as an absence of love. Or we might seek success because we believe it will bring us joy, and with each achievement we find ourselves despairing at the elusiveness of joy. Obviously there is nothing wrong with our characters wanting love, or wanting to be successful, but when they make meaning out of these goals they actually create the impossibility of achieving them. By exploring the meaning that our protagonist makes out of her goal, we begin to get a glimpse of her dilemma.

STORY MAXIM #4: Our protagonist does not rid himself of his desire, but when he reframes the meaning he makes out of his desire, he is no longer ruled by it.

EVERY STORY BEGINS WITH A FALSE BELIEF

Since the purpose of story is to reveal a transformation, the arc of the story moves from a place of not knowing to knowing. Whether the story illustrates the journey from fear to love, ignorance to wisdom, revenge to forgiveness, denial to acceptance, or some other journey, it is through the protagonist's false belief that our reader is led to a new understanding. It is not that our protagonist's belief is incorrect; it is just not the whole story. The protagonist's false belief is going to be tested through the story, and this will lead him to a new understanding. For example, in John Grisham's *The Firm*, the protagonist, Mitch McDeere, believes that money will solve his problems. He takes a well-paying job with a firm that he knows nothing about, and soon discovers that he is working for the mob and can never get out. It is true that money can solve some of his problems, but until he is willing to lose everything, he is a hostage to this false belief.

We tend to focus on our immediate problem rather than on its underlying cause. Let's say that our protagonist Bill has a few drinks at the bar, and while driving home he gets a DUI. At this point, he most assuredly has a problem, but underlying his problem may be a dilemma. Perhaps Bill is an alcoholic and wants to get sober but believes that he cannot survive the anxiety of sobriety. Although the problem may be the DUI and its attendant inconveniences, underlying this problem is the false belief that he cannot survive as a sober person. By noticing our character's desire coupled with his false belief, we begin to see the dilemma.

STORY MAXIM #5: By exploring the tension that drives any scene in our story, and delving into the internal struggle between the character's desire and the meaning she attaches to her desire, we are led to the dilemma.

EXAMPLES OF DILEMMAS FROM CONTEMPORARY NOVELS

Fight Club: The unnamed protagonist craves a sense of identity and belonging. However, he believes that he is incapable of making decisions for himself. The dilemma is resolved when he destroys his false self and takes responsibility for his life.

Eat, Pray, Love: The author and protagonist, Elizabeth Gilbert, seeks to enjoy the pleasures of the world while devoting herself to God. The dilemma is resolved when she reframes her relationship to "balance" by trusting her heart.

The English Patient: The protagonist, Count Laszlo de Almasy, wants to reveal himself, but believes that intimacy leads to suffering for himself and others. The dilemma is resolved when he reveals his story to Caravaggio, which leads to understanding and forgiveness.

ALL OF OUR CHARACTERS CONSTELLATE AROUND THE DILEMMA

Since story is the exploration of a theme, and theme is revealed through characters in conflict, every character in our story has a relationship to the dilemma. This does not mean that all of our characters are struggling with the dilemma in the same way, but that the dilemma is universal and it keeps our story anchored to its theme.

STORY MAXIM #6: Identify your protagonist's goal, and you will discover that all of your characters share this goal.

In *Fight Club*, the hero and Tyler Durden both want a sense of identity. In *The English Patient*, the characters all crave intimacy, and in *Eat, Pray Love*, all of the characters have a different relationship to "balance." If our protagonist wants revenge because he believes that it will set him free, we may notice that all of our characters are seeking freedom through a variety of approaches. If our protagonist wants success because he believes that it will provide him with a sense of validation, we may notice that all of our characters are seeking validation in different ways.

STORY MAXIM #7: The resolution to the protagonist's dilemma involves the shedding of her old identity.

Though liberating, transformation can be bittersweet, because there is always a cost attached. Something must be lost. Becoming an adult means the death of our youth. Falling in love means the death of singlehood. Having a child may herald the death of irresponsibility.

CHARACTER AND DILEMMA

The dilemma must be explored through character. If the characters' dilemma is not shown through action and conflict, it will have little effect on the reader. Regardless of race, religion, social class, or geography, every human being can relate to love, hate, pride, fear, trust, rage, compassion, impatience, self-pity, lust, faith, betrayal, and all other primal experiences.

A WIDER PERSPECTIVE

The purpose of inquiring into the dilemma is to gain a wider perspective on our story. I was working with a writer whose protagonist wanted desperately to protect the family legacy and was threatened by her daughter falling in love with a man of a different race. Although the writer's story was rich with conflict, she was unable to see how to resolve the mother's bitterness with her imagined ending of the mother accepting her daughter and future husband. How on earth could she bridge this intractable problem? The solution lay in inquiring into the nature of family legacy as opposed to her idea of it. The dilemma resolved itself when the mother reframed her relationship to her family's legacy and discovered that it was not about a bloodline, but about unconditional love.

The reason a well-told story is so compelling is because the reader understands implicitly that the protagonist is struggling with an unsolvable problem. As authors it is unlikely that we fully comprehend the dilemma in all of its manifestations, though we almost certainly have a *sense* of it. Exploring the dilemma is a process that continues in the rewrite. The same way that a photographer is not fully conscious of why she snaps the picture, there is a similar experience for writers. We are attempting to capture something on the page, a fleeting thought, an experience that we can not quite articulate, an idea that we do not quite understand, and by placing these moments in the context of a story, these experiences can be transmitted to our reader as something larger than we are, something beyond our limited understanding.

STORY STRUCTURE

Many novelists resist the idea of three-act structure because they fear it will limit their creativity and lead to formulaic writing. Story structure is not an equation designed to reduce our story to quantifiable parts. This misconception may be the result of structure being taught by story analysts whose gifts lean more toward an ability to deconstruct the anatomy of an existing work rather than in exploring the nature of the author's intention. This can leave the student with a keen understanding of how a particular story was "assembled," while struggling with how to translate the lesson into completing his or her own work. Although one might eventually begin to grasp the inner workings of structure by staring at the various "parts" of a story, there is perhaps a more direct approach.

Story structure is a paradigm for transformation. It is a way to trace the experiential beats of a character's growth that leads to his "shift in perception." A shift in perception, that *aha* experience that we have all had when we see something one way, and then in a flash, see it from an entirely different perspective, is miraculous, yet it is as common as dust bunnies. Transformation is an alchemical process; a caterpillar becomes a butterfly, coal becomes a diamond, a person falls in love. Through pressure, or conflict, an organism is distilled to its essence in order to become its truest self.

Without these three core elements a story cannot satisfy its premise:

1. Desire. (A character wants something.)

2. Surrender. (A character lets go of the possibility of achieving his goal.)
3. Transformation. (A character reframes his goal, thus seeing it from a new perspective.)

Story structure actually has little to do with plot. In fact, the "structure" that is being alluded to is actually the underlying theme. But what is a theme exactly, and how does working with it help us structure our work? As was just discussed, every character in our story has a relationship to a central dilemma, and it is through these various struggles that our theme is explored. By tracking our protagonist's desire or *goal* through the story, this dilemma is revealed.

Making a story is a process of moving from the general to the specific. We begin with a basic sense of a story, and through inquiry our imagination fills in the details of character and circumstance. By holding on tightly to any story element, we limit our story from moving in the direction of its most fully realized form.

Just as Elisabeth Kubler-Ross' seminal book *On Death and Dying* illustrates the five key experiences that one moves through in the grief process, there are a series of experiences that are essential in tracing our protagonist's arc that leads to his transformation. Although the five stages of grief may overlap, they tend to move in a particular direction: denial, anger, bargaining, depression, and finally acceptance. When we look at these experiences, we likely sense a certain internal logic to the process. In fact, if we ponder them, eventually our imagination is likely to begin conjuring a story!

We all have an empathetic imagination that allows us to connect to our common humanity. Just as the five stages of grief are universal, so are the key experiential stages that lead to our protagonist's transformation. It is the plot, the series of events that happen within the story, that provides a platform for these key experiential stages.

Notice that the five stages of grief cannot exist without an individual wanting something – namely, to live. Without a desire to live, there is nothing to be in denial of, nothing to be angry about, nothing to bargain for, nothing to be depressed about, and nothing to accept, because living never mattered in the first place. It is the same with our story. Our protagonist must want something, and the stakes must be life and death.

The reason for learning the fundamentals of story structure is to make the whole greater than the sum of its parts. We have all read novels that caught our interest with their premise, or the narrator's voice, yet ultimately did not amount to much. We know when something does not ring true. We may not be able to articulate it, but we can feel it. And there are instances where virtually every detail rings true, yet the story still does not fulfill its promise. The purpose of the structure questions at the back of the book is to hold our characters accountable to universal truths so that our ending is the culmination of all that preceded it.

There is a reason that Shakespeare's plays have been around for hundreds of years. Aside from the beauty of the language, they are, by and large, fiercely well-structured stories that plumb the depths of human experience. This is not to suggest that we should eschew experimentation. However, experimentation without an understanding of story structure is akin to finger-painting; we can fill up the whole page, but its value may be purely sentimental.

By exploring structure as an experiential journey we will discover how our first draft can become more dynamic and specific. This does not mean that the story necessarily needs to be re-plotted. It means that we are going to understand why we wrote what we wrote by becoming aware of what our subconscious did quite naturally.

It is important to note that just like life, no character exists in a vacuum. We affect each other, and every action produces a reaction. This means that as we track our protagonist through the story, he is continuously being affected by the various antagonists and vice versa. Each experience builds on the previous experience, thus the story gathers in meaning as it progresses. Without each experience, the next experience cannot exist. While the hero's goal never changes, through conflict his approach is constantly changing, which means that his journey is nonlinear.

For example:

- The journey to success includes failure.
- The journey to self-discovery includes confusion.
- The journey to love includes heartbreak.

The dilemma that our protagonist struggles with may well be precisely the one we are doing battle with in our own lives. This is because *the desire to write is the desire to evolve, or to resolve something we seek to understand.* I joke with my students that the difference between writing class and therapy is that in writing class we are guaranteed a transformation – all we have to do is imagine it. And it is true. By simply exploring the choice our protagonist makes between what he wants and what he needs, we begin to glimpse the resolution to the dilemma.

By exploring the key experiences in our hero's journey, we will discover moments that make our story more dynamic and help us see beyond our fixed idea of how the story ought to go. This does not mean that our story will go in an entirely different direction, but that through inquiry we will see our story from a wider perspective.

THE KEY EXPERIENCES
IN OUR HERO'S JOURNEY

ACT ONE

OPENING/FALSE BELIEF: Our hero wants something. Without a powerful want, there is no story. Until we have a sense of what our protagonist wants, we will be unclear on our throughline. Our protagonist also carries with him a false belief, a mistaken idea of himself and/or his world. Since the purpose of transformation is to reveal a wider perspective, the story often begins with a false belief that is founded on a set of incontestable facts, but as the story progresses, the interpretation of these facts evolves. For instance, in Cormac McCarthy's *The Road*, the man believes that the world is unsafe and that he must destroy anyone who crosses his path. In fact, he is prepared to kill his own son if he perceives that the boy might suffer at the hands of another. And he is right. The world is a post-apocalyptic nightmare, yet in the end the father is dead, and a family happens upon the boy and takes him into their fold. It most certainly is a dark and terrifying world, but it is not without hope, as the father initially believed.

DILEMMA: Our hero's desire is wrapped up in a false belief about what his goal actually means, which creates a dilemma. This dilemma is often called the dramatic problem of the story because it appears that he has a problem, but in fact, he has a dilemma. For example, a character may want love because he believes that it will complete him. Through the story he may learn that his desire for love actually prevents him from ever having it because as long as he believes that he requires love in order to feel complete he will be unable to accept that he is already complete. By introducing the hero's apparent "problem" early in the story, we understand the nature of his struggle in universal terms.

INCITING INCIDENT: This is sometimes called the "Why is this day unlike any other?" moment. Whether it is Toto's disappearance in *The Wizard of Oz*, or Katniss' sister being chosen as a tribute in *The Hunger Games*, something happens that causes our protagonist to respond, thus providing a context for the dilemma. It might originally have been universal, but now we understand how it is personal to the hero.

OPPOSING ARGUMENT: This is a moment somewhere in the middle or two-thirds of the way through Act One where an antagonist responds to our protagonist thus presenting the other side of the "apparent" problem. This moment is necessary because it illustrates the protagonist's specific dilemma. Until our reader understands the nature of the dilemma, as opposed to the appearance of the problem, there will be no context for his decision at the end of Act One. Conversely, it is only as a result of the Inciting Incident where our hero is galvanized to take action that the opposing argument is understood.

DECISION: At the end of Act One, our protagonist makes a decision that he cannot go back on toward achieving his goal. A decision that he cannot go back on may involve anything from telling a secret to proclaiming his love, to a first kiss, to moving across town, to agreeing to a promotion, to entering a wizardry academy. Notice the reluctance that precedes this decision. Without reluctance, we will not have a context for the dilemma.

ACT TWO

FALSE HOPE: Our hero achieves success toward achieving his goal. It appears that his goal is within reach. Without this moment we do not have a context for the meaning that he makes out of his goal. He is yet unaware of the conundrum facing him. If his desire is to be loved and he succeeds in getting a woman to fall for him, he is yet to confront the real problem, which may be the meaning that he has made out of her love. He has an idea of what his success should look like, but until he sheds the meaning that he has attached to it, he will be in bondage to his goal.

MIDPOINT – TEMPTATION: As a result of our hero's false hope, an event happens that causes our hero to respond through temptation. He is pulled in two different directions between what he wants and what he needs. He has come a long way and has made great strides, but now is faced with a crisis of conscience. He can take a shortcut or he can risk everything for his dream.

SUFFERING: My God, he had no idea it was going to be this difficult! If he had known he might never have begun this journey in the first place. The suffering is a direct result of the hero's dawning suspicion that what he wants is impossible to achieve, based upon the meaning he has attached to his goal. In other words, he senses that what he is facing is not a problem, but rather, a dilemma, which is impossible to solve. The suffering is the death rattle of our hero's old identity. He's going to give it one last try.

SURRENDER: We surrender when we run out of choices. The end of Act Two is where our protagonist recognizes the impossibility of ever achieving his goal, and he lets it go. The end of Act Two is like a coin with two sides. On one side is the dark night of the soul, and on the other side is a wider perspective. This is where he reframes his relationship to his goal.

ACT THREE

ACCEPTING REALITY: By reframing his relationship to his goal, he begins to accept the reality of his situation. There's a saying: The truth will set you free, but first it will kick your butt. That is where our hero is. He is getting his butt kicked, but it is leading him to a new understanding of how things really work.

BATTLE SCENE: This is the climax of our story where our hero makes a choice between what he wants and what he needs. This is an extremely difficult choice for the hero. Through this choice he proves to the gods that he has earned his transformation, and thus resolves the dilemma.

NEW EQUILIBRIUM: This is the ending of our story where our hero is returned home. How is he relating differently to the other characters in the story? What has he come to understand through his journey?

TECHNICAL MATTERS

What follows are technical matters to consider before beginning the 90-Day Rewrite. For every suggestion or example, there are always exceptions. Although there are no rules, the principles that follow will allow you to make informed choices in your work.

STORY

SHOW, DON'T TELL

We have all read the writing books that insist we "show and don't tell." This phrase can be misinterpreted as an imperative rather than a caution. *Showing* means that we are bringing our reader directly into the scene through exposition, description, dialogue and detail. There is an immediacy in showing that is absent in telling. *Telling* involves summarizing events and can feel distancing for the reader, as if the events are simply being reported.

However, there is a place for telling, and in fact, there are situations where it is preferable and even necessary to tell the events rather than show them. Not every piece of information in our story demands the same level of importance, thus at times it is beneficial to summarize selected events in order to focus on the drama that is crucial to the story.

For instance, if Bob and Larry are driving from New York to San Francisco to rob a bank and we need our reader to understand the rising tension between them, then a scene might be necessary to illustrate this dynamic. However, if we were to write every blessed moment of their drive, our reader would be stultified with boredom. Our reader is likely most interested in the "turning points," those moments when the relationship shifts through tension and conflict. By showing these moments, while sketching in or "telling" the events that lead to them, our reader will have a sense of the entire journey without the narrative flatlining.

Let's look at an example:

Bob stopped at a gas station in Denver and filled his tank. He paid the attendant in cash and climbed back into the car.

"That was forty bucks," he said to Larry. "You owe me twenty."

"Don't have any money."

Bob glanced at his partner. "I hope you're not expecting me to pay our way to California."

Larry shrugged. "I'll pay you back when the job's done."

Bob drove in silence for nearly an hour. When he finally spoke, he said, "I think I'll pull over at the next stop. Feel free to watch me eat my dinner."

Larry smiled. He reached into his pocket and riffled through a wad of cash. "I'm getting hungry myself."

The short opening paragraph where Bob stops at the gas station is "telling," but it is necessary to provide context for the scene that follows. We don't really need to know if Bob filled up the car with regular or unleaded, or what the temperature was in Denver, or the gender of the attendant. Although these details could be included, it is important to recognize the point of tension in the scene, and to direct our focus to that area. Toward the end of the passage, where Bob drives in silence for nearly an hour, there is another moment of telling that acts as a bridge between the next scene where the tension mounts as Larry reveals that he's lied about not having any cash.

Sometimes telling can go on for pages when the tension is high. Our reader may need a break from the drama, and this is where we can introduce *backstory* that deepens the reader's understanding of the characters and their motives.

Revealing information is called *exposition*. Sometimes information is revealed through the narrator telling it to the reader, but it is also possible to dramatize exposition as well.

Let's say that Nick's mother has just died and that he has gone to the bar to drown his sorrows. His father, with whom his relationship was strained, died a few years back, and now Nick is struggling to make sense of this loss. Rather than simply telling the reader this information, we can search for creative ways to infuse it into a scene. For instance:

Paddy placed two shots of whiskey on the bar. He raised a glass and said, "To your sweet Mum, may she rest in peace."

The two men downed their drinks.

Nick stared into his glass and shook his head, "It wasn't like this when Pa died."

"When you lose your father, you become a man," said Paddy, pouring two more shots.

Nick swallowed hard. "And when you lose your Mum?"

Paddy threw back the whiskey and set the glass back on the bar. "Ay, that's when you become an orphan."

REPETITION

In our real lives we repeat patterns of behavior ad infinitum, but in fiction, if the events do not contribute to the story by building in meaning, we may lose our reader's interest. Let's say that Jimbo is a smoker, and one day he decides to quit. He stops smoking for a week, and then he starts again. Six months later, he does the same thing, and this pattern continues for twenty years. Unless the story is an examination of the myriad reasons one quits smoking only to pick it back up, it is unlikely that our reader will be interested in each aborted attempt at abstinence. The significance for our reader lies not in the stopping and starting, but in the underlying meaning that this pattern connotes.

As readers, we tend to be more interested in what particular moments mean than we are in revisiting similar moments again and again. This is not to suggest that we should not show repetitive behaviors in our work, but that we place our focus on the reason for the repetition in order to convey its underlying meaning.

Repetition can happen at the level of behavior, and also of information. If Tom tells Woody the story of how he grew up in an orphanage, and later meets Jenny, we do not want to have to sit through him telling her the exact same story. If Jenny needs to know this crucial information in order to move the story forward, there are ways for her to find out. He can begin to tell her, and the rest can happen "offstage," or he can tell her in an entirely different way, thus altering the meaning of what he told Tom, thereby shifting the reader's perspective.

COINCIDENCE VERSUS SYNCHRONICITY

Readers typically do not like coincidences in fiction. Sure, coincidences occur in our lives every day, but in stories they can present a problem. Readers lose interest when coincidence leans in the protagonist's favor because *convenience does not convey meaning.* Character is revealed through conflict. For example, if Biff is hitchhiking on a deserted road, trying to get to Chicago for a wedding, and he is picked up by Chuck, the best man, who just happens to be passing by – that is a coincidence. But if Biff is thumbing it to Chicago and just happens to be picked up by the husband of the woman he's having an affair with – that is synchronistic. *Synchronicity conveys meaning,* while coincidence does not. Coincidence lacks conflict. It is expedient, and often an indication of where the writer got stuck and tried to force the plot forward. Rather than searching for a creative solution, the writer simply creates a convenient situation in order to keep the story moving forward. Synchronicity speaks to the underlying meaning of the author's intent. There's a reason for the particular event, which raises the stakes.

If we find ourselves relying on coincidence to move our story forward, let's explore ways to disguise it by creating conflict that is germane to our theme. It does not mean that we need to ditch our idea of Chuck giving Biff a ride, but we might want to inquire into why this ride will be more trouble than either character had bargained for. We can keep our story points – as long as we lose, or disguise, the coincidences.

PACING AND PROPORTION

Pacing is something that is forever in flux. There is pacing at the level of sentence, paragraph, chapter and act. As we work through our prose, our book will reveal to us its natural rhythm. The challenge with pacing can be that as one section is altered, it can influence the pacing of the entire manuscript. This is why we are going to do an outline in Week One, before beginning our actual rewrite. It is difficult to have objectivity about the entire story when we are busily refining a specific passage in the manuscript, but by getting the lay of the land prior to the rewrite, we will be better equipped to have a sense of how our story wants to be paced.

Our reader is always subconsciously searching for meaning. We must be aware of this, otherwise there can be a tendency to place importance on something that does not carry much weight, while breezing past events of paramount significance. If there is a moment in our story that is a key turning point, it likely deserves more than a sentence, while rewarding a relatively minor moment or insight it with its own lengthy chapter will imbue it with a sense of importance that can distract the reader from our story's larger meaning.

DELAYING INFORMATION

Some people consider it manipulative for an author to *delay* or *withhold* information from the reader, while the question we ought to ask ourselves is: "What is the most effective way to tell my story?"

Whatever it takes to produce the most emotionally and intellectually satisfying experience for our reader is valid. Let's say that we are writing a story in which we have introduced a character who has been paroled for committing a terrible crime, and he meets a newly single woman smarting from her failed romance, and they begin to fall in love. Perhaps the woman is aware that he is on parole but does not want to know what he did because she is using the relationship to avoid her broken heart. Even though the author knows his crime, in order to create tension, he might choose to withhold the information and reveal it at the same time that the woman discovers the truth. If he were to tell the reader of his crime, the story would be an entirely different experience and might lack a narrative drive.

In every story, the writer must make decisions about when and how to reveal information. These decisions influence the story's tone, pace and even its interpretation. As authors, we have a multitude of choices and need not feel bogged down by having to reveal information simply because we have hinted at it. On the other hand, to allow our reader to get ahead of the story can be fatal. If our reader knows what is coming, and particularly if she is guessing correctly at information that we have withheld, then we are not doing our job. Reading is the one occasion where it is actually thrilling to have our hopes dashed and our expectations defied.

By noticing the places where we build tension by withholding information, we can ask ourselves whether we are actually raising the stakes, or whether we are causing our reader to roll his eyes because what we are foreshadowing is just plain obvious.

DEUS EX MACHINA

Deus ex machina means "an act of God," and is a term used to describe a story that ends with a tidy solution arriving from seemingly out of nowhere. If our ending is not intrinsic to the thematic elements that preceded it, it will likely seem forced and our reader may feel robbed of a satisfying ending.

Our protagonist's dilemma can only truly be resolved through a shift in perception, and a *deus ex machina* ending can cheat our reader out of that experience. If all that happens in our story is that our protagonist gets what he wants, our reader will be disappointed. Our reader is interested in him getting what he needs in order to reveal a deeper meaning. This means: no tidal waves wiping out the bad guys, no deathbed confessions telling the hero where the treasure is hidden, and no sudden revelations from our hero that have not been foreshadowed and woven into the fabric of the narrative.

To avoid a *deus ex machina* ending, we must return to our theme, and trust that it is valid. Our characters are in service to this theme, and by revisiting the story structure questions we can investigate how our story can lead to its most dynamic conclusion.

CHARACTER AND CONFLICT

It is important to note that at their core, our characters all want the same thing, because they are all functions of the theme. Whether it is love, revenge, freedom, control, forgiveness, or one of a hundred other primal motives, the desire is shared because it is through this desire that our theme is explored. The want may be the same; however, their approaches toward getting it may differ wildly. By distilling our characters' primary desire, we will begin to see this similarity, and will be led to our theme.

ANTAGONISTS

It is through conflict with our *antagonists* that our protagonist is transformed. Without powerful antagonists there will be no transformation. Our protagonist cannot overcome his antagonists through force of will. If he could, he would. Our antagonists are more powerful, more stubborn, more ruthless, and more cunning than our protagonist. Oftentimes what separates our protagonist from our antagonist is that our protagonist is willing to surrender the meaning that he made out of his goal. It is through understanding his true situation that our protagonist develops wisdom and is able to see his situation from a wider perspective. Wisdom trumps power, ruthlessness and cunning. By seeing things in a new way, it becomes possible for our protagonist to get what he wants, if what he wants belongs in his life.

Writers sometimes ask me, "What if my antagonist is a force or a concept?" or "What if my hero is his own antagonist?" Yes, these things are possible, and may likely be the case. However, conflict arises through action. If our antagonist is conceptual, we must make sure that we can show how this force manifests itself in preventing the protagonist from achieving his goal.

Lastly, our hero is always struggling with an internal false belief. In that respect, he certainly carries within himself an antagonistic force, but that does not make him the antagonist. It simply gives him an inner struggle to overcome.

DESCRIBING CHARACTERS' FEELINGS

Feelings are subjective. If we write "Bill felt despondent" or "Jane was happy," we must be curious about how we can show these experiences through *action*. Our reader does not particularly care what our characters are feeling. She is interested in how they react and respond to other characters. When we become lost in the enormity of our characters' feelings, we may assume that the feelings alone will provide a context for what is happening in the story. They will not. It is through a series of actions and reactions that character is revealed.

PSYCHOLOGICAL MOTIVES

The same goes for explaining characters' *psychological motives*. By illustrating the conflict, our reader will understand what led the character to become who he is. Rather than telling us that Bill is in denial, we can explore ways to show through action how Bill's denial manifests itself, or how Sally comes to confront her dark past, or how Tom's thought processes led him to a life of crime. Explaining a character's psychological motivation can be a shortcut for showing through action the reasons for his decisions. We will understand his psychological makeup through his response to situations.

CHARACTERS ARE A FUNCTION OF OUR STORY

Each one of our characters performs a function. Our reader unconsciously understands this and will be confused if a character's function remains unclear. She will wonder what this character has to do with the story as a whole. Sometimes we create characters as a way to distract ourselves from the primary conflict.

Does our protagonist need to have seventeen siblings in order for our reader to understand that she comes from a large family? If we are going to introduce all seventeen siblings, let's make sure that their roles are intrinsic to the story. Five is a huge family when there are few resources and little love. An only child can feel as invisible as a kid raised with a dozen siblings, just as a kid with many siblings can feel like the most doted-on child in the world.

CONFLATING CHARACTERS

Sometimes we have written characters that do not belong in our story because their function is redundant. The character may be engaged in conflict that does not add anything new to the story. If we find ourselves wondering why a character is in our story, and we are unclear on what his function is, it is possible that he does not belong. When we imagine removing him from the story, does it tighten the narrative? Or is it possible that he serves a crucial function, but a function that might be better served through another character? We can always conflate characters by distilling one character's function and giving the necessary traits and situations to another character in the story.

Let's say that we have written a story where Kyle and Patty are dealing with the aftermath of a divorce. If we write about a second couple, George and Sandy, and have them dealing with the same issues in a fairly similar way, we might ask ourselves what the purpose of George and Sandy's divorce is in the story. Does it advance the story? Does it offer something new and meaningful to our theme? Just because the specific events surrounding their divorce may differ, if there is not a specific reason for introducing them, the reader will likely be confused by the second couple's presence. However, if George and Sandy's relationship to their divorce is significantly different than Kyle and Patty's, and if their struggle provides new meaning, then it is likely that their function in the story is necessary.

There is value in going through our story and searching for characters whose roles feel similar to other characters, as their presence can sometimes confuse our reader.

CHARACTER NAMES

The sound and feel of our characters' names can convey worlds about our story. Names like Hannibal Lecter, Jane Eyre, Jay Gatsby, and Missus Malaprop conjure images that have entered our collective consciousness. The name Frankenstein means something quite different to us than Holden Caulfield.

Unless we are doing it intentionally, let us give our characters names that distinguish them from each other in the story. If our characters are named Don, Dawn, and Dan, our reader will be confused. By choosing names that vary in syllable and length, and are distinctive, or convey character through the use of hard or soft consonants, alliteration, and a variety of sounds, we may discover names that best suit our purposes.

Names can convey race, class, economic status, and even a

sense of humor. To name a character Kate means something different than naming her Daisy, and Tom means something different than Sheldon.

The names we choose are in service to our story. If our sweet, plain kindergarten teacher character is named Candy Darling, we have hopefully employed some irony into the text. If our gruff, burly construction worker is named Joseph Predwinkle Edwards III and insists on being addressed as such, there better be a darn good reason, otherwise our reader will be left scratching his head.

PROSE

BUILDING SENTENCES

There are no rules that limit the length of a sentence, but when our sentences are strung together by a variety of actions, the sentence can begin to strain credibility. What is wrong with the following sentence?

"Sally ran up the stairs, went into her bathroom, and brushed her teeth."

It is not possible that all of those things happened at once. Watch out for three or more events in a sentence. Writers sometimes try to cram so much into a sentence that one can almost feel the sentence laboring under the weight.

Try this. "Sally ran up the stairs to her bathroom. She stood at the sink and brushed her teeth."

If we are trying to show the instantaneousness of a situation, the following sentence might work just fine:

"Paul flew to Japan, got off the plane, and found a job."

However, if we have simply strung actions together in the hope that we are quickening the narrative – we are not. Though this is quite common, and we will see it in almost every department store bestseller, it is sloppy writing.

ADJECTIVES

Too many adjectives can mean that the writer is not in command of his story. Beware of the desire to emphasize, breathlessly proclaim, or add multiple details. Detail is different than specificity. Rid your work of all unnecessary adjectives.

How could the following sentence be simplified?

"John purchased the colossal many-roomed, red-bricked colonial mansion from Raymond, a rotund, bespectacled, thin-lipped, Midwestern, Communist, jazz vocalist."

What is lost if we wrote it as follows?

"John purchased the Colonial mansion from Raymond, a rotund, Communist jazz singer from Kansas City?"

TENSES

Are we writing our story in the past or present tense?
Past tense is:

"He ran to the store."

Present tense is:

"He runs to the store."

Most stories tend to be written in past tense, even if what is happening is in the present. What is important in the rewrite is to make sure that the tense does not change.

POINT OF VIEW

There are basically four points of view that a story can be told from: First person, second person, third person limited, and third person omniscient.

First person is a story told from the "I" perspective. "I woke up this morning to discover that I was a werewolf." Writing a story from first person has its advantages. There is an intimacy and immediacy in the narrator's voice as she speaks directly to the reader. She can tell us her most intimate thoughts and there can be a rich interior dialogue. The downside is that we are not privy to actions and happenings outside of her purview. She can only tell us what she is seeing and hearing. Thus, first-person narrative tends to work better for smaller stories. It is unusual, though not impossible for an epic to be told from the first-person perspective.

Second person is a story told from the "You" perspective. "You woke up this morning and wondered who that person was sleeping next to you." Although this perspective is rarely used, it was employed successfully in Jay McInerney's novel *Bright Lights, Big City*. It can be disorienting, as if the reader is being told intimate details of his own life, which may be why it was so effective in his tale of a young man who loses connection to himself through drugs and alcohol.

Third person limited (aka "third person close"), is told from the "He" or "She" perspective of one or more characters. "He woke up to discover that he was alone." Writing from the third person has its own advantages. The author can climb into the heads of various characters and describe what they are seeing and experiencing. A third-person narrative affords the author a wider canvas on which to tell her story.

Third person omniscient is the narrator that sees all. Omniscient literally means, "having infinite knowledge." This voice tends to be more factual in tone, as if the events are being reported from a detached source. The omniscient narrator was far more common in the nineteenth century before film and television. With the advent of a cinematic language, we have been conditioned to shift perspective rapidly, hence the rise in popularity of the third person-limited perspective.

Oftentimes in story the perspective can shift from third person omniscient to third person limited, in the same way that a film can go from a master shot to a close-up. The *omniscient point of view* might describe or give an overall picture of a situation before focusing on a particular character or situation through which the events can be relayed.

There are no rules to choosing our story's point of view. It is not uncommon in our first draft to switch points of view between first and third. Sometimes writers feel too close to their story in the first draft, and when the writing feels too personal, they switch to third person. In this instance, it is worth considering a first-person perspective for the rewrite. In another instance, the story might have so many third-person perspectives that it becomes clear that a first-person voice cannot contain the story. In this case, it is worth considering switching any first-person narration to a third-person perspective.

DIALOGUE

The goal of *dialogue* is to convey meaning and to move the story forward, while providing the illusion that these are real people talking. If we were to recount most conversations verbatim, we might risk putting our reader to sleep. The illusion of conversation is very different than actual conversation.

It is a sign that our writing has become general when dialogue is separated by lines that describe the passage of time. Instead of writing, "Bob sat for a very long time," or "Janet paused a moment before responding," we might consider pulling our reader directly into the moment by using description. What does the room look like? What is Bob doing? What does Janet stare at before responding? By transporting our reader into the moment, our work may become more alive and specific.

ADVERBS

"I hope I'm not late for dinner," he said, nervously.
"You are late for dinner," she said, angrily.

If a writer needs to tell us *how* a character is speaking, it is an indication that the dialogue lacks specificity. Of course, this is not a rule, and it is perfectly fine to use the occasional adverb. However *adverbs are not the most effective tool to communicate meaning.* Be specific, and look for ways to take the reader directly into the moment, such as the following:

"I hope I'm not late for dinner," he said.
"Not at all." She squeezed his arm and guided him into the dining room. The table was cleared, and a soufflé lay melting on the carpet, where their cat, Spike, licked at its remains. "You're right on time."

By finding ways to show the character's experience in relation to the dialogue, the adverb becomes redundant.

ON THE NOSE DIALOGUE

If the reader cannot cull the meaning from the dialogue itself, then it may not be clear enough. The line "You are late for dinner" is what is often referred to as "on-the-nose" dialogue, which means that there is no difference between what is being spoken and its intended meaning. In other words, there is no subtext. On-the-nose dialogue is flat and boring because it does not convey meaning, nor does it reveal character. Even if we are writing about some matter-of-fact, humorless Swiss accountant, there still must be something going on underneath his words.

Because in life there is virtually always subtext in dialogue!

By being aware of our characters' desires, and the immediate obstacles preventing them from achieving their goals, our reader will understand our characters through the words we put in their mouths.

Let's say that the couple has been dating for three months, and although she's quite attracted to the guy, she's fed up with him always being late. And perhaps he has accused her of having a terrible temper and so she is trying to contain her rage at his tardiness. They are both struggling with obstacles, and her "Not at all" line is understood to be passive-aggressive in light of the soufflé lying on the floor.

NAMES IN DIALOGUE

How often do we use people's names in real life? Rarely. Perhaps we use their names when we greet them and again when we say good-bye, but even that is uncommon. When we are angry with someone, or emphatic, we might be inclined to speak that person's name, but again, it is far less frequent than we might think.

Here is an example of dialogue using names:

"Bill, what are you doing here?"
"Just dropping off some files, Steve."

Sounds clunky, right? Now let's take the names out:

"What are you doing here?"
"Just dropping off some files."

If we are going to use names in our dialogue, let's make sure we are clear on our reason.

WEIGHTS AND MEASURES

PROXIMITY

Do our characters have to be two thousand miles apart, or three miles apart? If we are trying to convey a sense of distance, remember that *distance is relative.* Let's say that our protagonist lives in Los Angeles while her mother lives in Akron. In the first draft, the mother flits in and out of her life while also holding down a full-time job in her hometown. The story might feel burdensome with the characters either engaged in long phone conversations or flying back and forth. Unless the true distance is germane to the story, we might ask why we have placed the mother on the other side of the country. Is it because this is where our own mother actually lives? Fiction writers frequently pull the *wrong details* from their lives. Perhaps the mother feels that she lives too far away, while the daughter feels that she's too close. Perhaps the author felt this when her mother was living in Akron, but when she puts this into a story, the reader does not experience a sense of the mother's intrusion. When we look at what we are attempting to express we will find a sense of proximity that best suits our story.

MEASUREMENTS OF TIME AND DISTANCE

It is important when using *measurements of time and distance* to not assume that our reader understands the context. Running a mile means different things to different people. To write "He stood fifty yards from the tiger," could indicate danger or a lack of danger. What does it mean specifically for the character? Unless we provide our reader with context, its meaning will be lost.

To say, "Gloria stood five foot five," does not necessarily mean anything. Although writers do this all the time, objective descriptions without a little authorial guidance will confuse our reader. What is the author's reason for telling us her height? Is there something we are to cull from this description? Will her height affect the plot later on? Let's look for ways to tell our reader through description something that adds meaning to our story. For example: "Gloria was of average height, average weight and average intelligence. The only thing that wasn't average about her was that she was the daughter of Johnny Chance, the world's fastest go-cart driver."

MEMOIR/CREATIVE NONFICTION

Memoir isn't journaling. We are not interested in simply re-counting facts. The facts require a context. What do we want our reader to understand through these characters and situations? What does our protagonist come to understand through his journey? If we are not clear on why we are telling the story, our reader will not be either.

MEMORY VERSUS IMAGINATION

I often hear memoirists complain that they cannot remember exactly how an event happened. It is true that memory is selective and unreliable. However, we can depend upon our imagination to contextualize the event in order to serve our theme. This does not mean that we "make it up" but rather that we trust in the validity of our perception. The truth is subjective, and facts can be interpreted in a variety of ways, but until we have written down our perception of the events, there will be nothing with which to work. Sometimes, through the act of writing down our perception, we begin to understand the events in a new way.

Just because our parents or siblings remember a situation differently does not mean that our perception is invalid. We must trust our instincts to tell our story. The purpose of memoir is to interpret the facts in a way that explores a theme.

The desire to write is the desire to evolve. Occasionally, a writer may discover that his loved ones are ambivalent about his creative aspirations, because change is threatening. Although it may be unconscious, they may have all sorts of fears, such as feeling left behind, or like they will no longer be able to relate to the writer. It is important to be aware of this dynamic so that we do not let it stand in the way of our writing. The desire to tell the truth is always valid, even if we are not sure what that truth is.

PART TWO

the 90-day rewrite

WEEK ONE

A NEW OUTLINE

Now that we are familiar with the basic technical matters, our goal this week is to create a new outline. If it seems strange to simply be re-outlining something that we have already written, that is not what we are doing. Rather, we are allowing ourselves to imagine the most compelling version of our story, which may contain large swaths of existing material, but also material yet to be written. Our first draft is likely quite different than the story we originally imagined, and through the rewrite process we will continue to refine our intentions. This does not mean that our outline will be a completely different story. It just means that before we get into the minutiae of our prose, it is valuable to step back and see the big picture in order to explore the most effective way to tell our story.

QUESTIONS FOR THE WEEK

1. What do I want to express through this story?

2. What is the most effective order of events to express it?

3. Do I have a worthy antagonist?

4. Am I dramatizing the story through action, or am I simply telling the reader what happens?

5. What is at stake for my protagonist?

6. Can I track my protagonist's want through the story points?

7. Am I sure that my protagonist is, in fact, my protagonist? Is it possible that another character in my story has a more dynamic arc?

8. Are there any moments or scenes that do not seem to belong in the story? Does removing them tighten the narrative drive?

9. Are there scenes that feel redundant, but contain essential information? Can I conflate these scenes and put the essential information somewhere else?

10. Are there characters that feel similar to other characters in the story, yet still perform one or two important functions? Is it possible to give these functions to another character?

11. Am I noticing how the dilemma is alive through every scene in the story, and how it is explored in different ways through each story point?

REWRITE MANTRA

My book is a work in progress. By maintaining a spirit of curiosity, everything I write, rewrite and edit either belongs, or is leading me to what ultimately belongs in my story. I am uniquely qualified to write this story, and through this process I will not abdicate authority over my work to anyone, including agents, publishers, family or friends. This does not mean that at some point I will not ask for feedback, but I will not make changes without first checking with myself that the changes serve what I am attempting to express, even if I am not able to articulate it. My impulses and hunches are precious assets. If one's critical opinion does not ring true, regardless of the source, I will disregard it. I trust that what I am expressing is valid because my impulses are valid.

DAY 1

"For the novels I wrote before selling anything, I didn't outline much. I had a vague idea of the story."
—GEORGE STEPHEN

ONCE MORE, WITH FEELING

Hi Writers,

Our goal this week is to clarify our story by rewriting our outline. Take three sheets of paper and write Act One, Act Two, and Act Three at the tops of the respective pages. Describe the plot in brief bullet points. Be sure to track your protagonist's motivation through each story point. You will find three pages with story points at the end of today's letter. And you will find the story structure questions to guide you through this outline at the back of the book.

As we reread our outlines, let's ask ourselves how we can enrich the drama by exploring the conflict between our protagonist and antagonists. Our job is to keep it alive while exploring new possibilities that will both enliven and clarify what we have already written.

When we feel that we have a basic confidence in our story, we can begin transcribing. If our story is already on the computer, we can begin rereading the first act and cutting sections we know do not belong, either because they are redundant, or they editorialize, i.e., explicitly tell rather than dynamically show the reader what is going on. Let's be diligent about finding unique ways to dramatize the conflict, rather than relying too heavily on exposition. We may discover that our story becomes more immediate, alive, and immersive.

Our story reveals itself gradually; each part informs the next. Every aspect of our story is inextricably linked, a reality that may lead us to making changes in Act Two or Act Three while focusing on Act One.

There are no hard and fast rules in this process.

Sometimes we can spend a lot of time refining a scene that does not end up in our novel. Of course, this process is by no means a science, and no time spent writing is ever wasted, but keep in mind that we are after a certain efficiency in this process. It might serve us to have a basic confidence in our new outline before we dive headlong into rewriting scenes that we are not quite sure belong.

TODAY
Using the structure questions at the back of the book, write a point-form outline of your story on the following three pages.

Until tomorrow,
Al

ACT ONE

Opening/False Belief

Dilemma

Inciting Incident

Opposing Argument

Hero Makes a Decision

ACT TWO

Our Hero Enters the New World

Our Hero Experiences False Hope

Midpoint: Our Hero Experiences Temptation

Our Hero's New Relationship to Antagonist

Our Hero Suffers

Our Hero Surrenders

ACT THREE

Our Hero Accepts the Reality of His Situation

Our Hero Takes Action

The Battle Scene

Our Hero Returns Home

DAY 2

"The first draft reveals the art. Revision reveals the artist."
               —MICHAEL LEE

HOLD IT LOOSELY

Hi Writers,

Writing our first draft was an instinctual process. The rewrite requires that we exercise different creative muscles, and yet, just as in the first draft, we need to maintain some distance from our story so that it can be bigger than we are. When we step back and ask, "Where did that come from?" we are often led to a deeper understanding of our story.

We can maintain this distance by holding our story loosely. We all have a bullshit detector. We need to continually ask ourselves, "Am I just writing this because I need to move the story forward, or is this true to my characters?"

Writing is hard work. We get tired. We want to be done. We think, "Oh, no one will notice." The fact is, writing requires both time and patience. If we sit with our story and sincerely inquire, we will be rewarded with the truth.

ORDER OF EVENTS

An effective order of events is crucial to writing the strongest, most compelling version of our story. It may not play out exactly as we had imagined it, but that is actually a good thing, because our story builds as complications are revealed. The perpetual unresolved desire besetting our hero is constant throughout the story, yet even that becomes more interesting as the edited and rewritten story becomes more nuanced.

Let's continue to explore how we can structure our story in the most compelling way. We may discover that we are thinking in a less linear way, that our opening may actually contain information and even characters that did not exist in the first draft.

Let's pay particular attention to our opening. Every story begins with "Why is this day unlike any other?" Something happens that sets the story into motion. There is crucial information that must be revealed in order for the reader to understand the *meaning* of why this day is unlike any other. The opening provides a context for our inciting incident.

TODAY

Consider the following questions as you re-imagine the opening of your book up to the inciting incident:

1. Does the reader understand clearly why this day is unlike any other?
2. Does the reader understand the dilemma? Is it universally relatable?
3. Is there crucial information that still needs to be revealed?
4. Is there any information that can be revealed later?
5. Where can I tighten the prose?
6. Where am I being redundant?

Until tomorrow,
Al

DAY 3

*"Writing and rewriting are a constant search for what
it is one is saying."*   —JOHN UPDIKE

TRUSTING OURSELVES

Hi Writers,

Storytelling is an art, not a science. We cannot approach our story
as if it were a math problem. If something is puzzling us, apply-
ing hard logic rarely helps. We must go deeper and inquire into the
seemingly counterintuitive impulses that continually arise. Writing
is a process of being willing to follow patterns and lines of thought,
even as they may sometimes turn into dead ends. By letting go of
the expectation that every session must bear rich fruit, we relax and
we do not burn out so easily.

Our story is about something beyond plot. Our subconscious
has made all sorts of connections in the first draft that speak directly to the dilemma at the heart of our story. In the rewrite, we
are being invited to make these connections conscious, to create
something more than a sensorial experience for our reader. We are
the only person who can *truly* know what our story is about. Sort
of terrifying, isn't it? Because even we are not quite sure what it is
about, at least not entirely. And we never will be, because we are
simply channels for what wants to be told through us.

Our creative work is in some ways a byproduct of our own
growth. The confusion and discomfort we may experience *is part*

of the work. It is a necessary experience in order to understand our story in a more specific way. We are creating a document that says, *"Here is what I know to be true."* Why would we want to subcontract this task out to someone less qualified?

If we are willing to sit with the confusion and occasional panic, and to show up to do our daily work, we will be rewarded with insight. Usually it comes in dribs and drabs, but sometimes the insights will explode like geysers, and we will think, "My God, of course! How could I have not have seen this before?"

When we seek outside opinions, we interrupt this process and put our work at risk of losing clarity. We are essentially saying, "I don't believe the story really lives fully and completely within me. I don't believe I am really able to do this."

No one knows better than you.

TODAY

As you continue exploring your outline, notice a passage or section that doesn't quite feel like it is working, yet there is something you are unwilling to part with. Choosing only one sentence from the section, rewrite it with a new alternative. By doing this, you are able to see the section from a new perspective. What does it reveal?

Until tomorrow,
Al

DAY 4

"The purpose of narrative is to present us with complexity and ambiguity."   —SCOTT TUROW

NARRATIVE DRIVE

Hi Writers,

As we explore our outline, it is inevitable that there are moments where our story feels flat. Here are some questions we can ask ourselves to get our story back into gear:

1. What does my protagonist want?

2. What is my protagonist's dilemma?

3. What is happening at this moment in the story that is urgent?

4. What will happen if my hero does not get what he wants?

5. Why does this moment belong in my story?

6. Can I be more specific about what I am trying to say?

7. Does this scene belong somewhere else?

8. Can I distill what is essential in this scene and layer it into an existing scene?

9. Do I honestly understand what I am saying, or do I just think it sounds good?

Sometimes writing the first draft can feel like running an Olympic sprint. We are going as fast as we can, trying to get to the end before we have too much time to think. It is common in the rewrite to discover passages where we were bounding toward some deep truth, only to witness our idea evaporate into the mist. The revision process is where we shed what does not belong so that our story can reveal itself.

When we are feeling stuck, we can turn to the questions above. We can boil a cup of tea, clutch our red pencil and eliminate what is not working or what does not belong, even when those passages represent some of our "best writing." If our writing is not in service to the story, regardless of its charm, it may not belong in our book.

Sometimes we do not quite understand what our story is about, yet we sense that something valid wants to be expressed. Often what *appears* to be going on is a smokescreen. Be curious about the subtext of each action, and have faith that there are big ideas in your work, even if they are not yet clear.

For example, I will work with a writer who has had the story churning in his brain for years, and over time has developed some fixed ideas on what his story is about. But upon further inquiry he may discover that underneath the *apparent* conflict is an intractable inner struggle for the protagonist that drastically raises the stakes.

If there is conflict in our story, it is never wrong. Allow a moment of conflict to help you understand the dilemma in a different or more specific way. For example, my current work in progress examines a widower's experience of both guilt and grief in the aftermath of his wife's death. He is stricken with guilt at the knowledge that she was aware of his affair. He believes that only his dead wife can offer him forgiveness. His dilemma is that the more he seeks forgiveness, the more he confronts its impossibility. However, in a later scene, he argues with his friend, convincing him to make a meaningful film. They are wrestling with their legacies and what their lives will mean when they are gone.

As I write it, I return to my idea of the dilemma. I do not ever try to force a scene to fit my idea of the dilemma. Rather, as I read over my work, I analyze how each new addition relates to the dilemma at large. The goal is never to force, but to understand, and in understanding, the work can become clarified.

When I refrain from attempting to force my work to fit into my narrow idea of what it should be, I am invited to a more specific relationship to my theme. Forgiveness and legacy – what do these two things have to do with one another? This is the question that my subconscious is seeking to resolve. Perhaps forgiving oneself is, in fact, a necessary act in making a contribution to the world, or in freeing oneself so that one can. Perhaps we are already forgiven, and the idea of needing forgiveness from someone else might actually be faulty – maybe true forgiveness can only come from ourselves.

Hmm, interesting.

All of these ideas arise from inquiring into the connection between forgiveness and legacy.

The story lives fully and completely within us. The desire to write is the desire to resolve something that we seek to understand. By inquiring into the nature of the conflict we are connecting to an emotional throughline as opposed to an intellectualized idea of the plot.

Again, it is by inquiring into those ineffable impulses that we are led to a deeper understanding of our story. Inquiring does not mean "figuring it out." By exploring the relationship between two seemingly disparate elements, our subconscious guides us toward a more specific relationship to our story.

TODAY
Explore your protagonist's dilemma through each scene in your outline. Notice how your protagonist's goal or desire never changes, while her approach to getting what she wants is constantly changing.

Until tomorrow,
Al

DAY 5

"If there's a book you really want to read, but it hasn't been written yet, then you must write it."

—TONI MORRISON

WRITING FOR OUR IDEAL READER

Hi Writers,

Good storytelling demands that we be aware of our ideal reader. A certain objective detachment allows us to see what others will see. In the first draft, we let it rip and lost ourselves in the muse. But now, we must prepare to become ruthless editors, distilling our prose and clarifying our story's intention.

The process of telling a story is akin to a spacecraft moving toward planet Earth. As it approaches, it sees the Earth in increasingly greater detail. Our story began as a single idea, followed by a more specific imagining of the world. From there we wrote an outline, and then hammered out a messy first draft. Now that we have "channeled" a complete version of that initial story, we step back and consider the most effective way to tell it. Let's imagine for a moment that we are a typical reader. We come to a book with certain expectations. We want to be taken on a journey, to be cast under the storyteller's spell.

The accomplished storyteller approaches his story as a seduction. It should appear effortless and natural, never rushed, never pushing an agenda. How does one accomplish this? It is a combination of continually returning to the structure questions, while staying open to our *source*, that primal impulse that spoke to us in the first place.

By continually inquiring into the structure questions we develop an abiding relationship to the infinite complexities of our characters. By being open, we become surprised at the unpredictability of human behavior. It is our job to ask ourselves in moments of crisis or doubt, "I wonder where this experience lives in the world of my characters?" Rather than getting swallowed up by our own guilt, fear or neurosis, let's explore how we are uniquely qualified to write our book.

Notice also that as our story progresses it builds in meaning. Our story is about something beyond the plot. In Mario Puzo's *The Godfather,* Michael Corleone begins the story as a soldier returning from war, a man who sees his life entirely separate from his corrupt mafia family, but by the end of the story he has taken over the family business. It is the meaning that Puzo wrings from this plot that gives the story its resonance. We experience the agony of Michael's dilemma as he becomes increasingly torn between his love for Kay and his loyalty to family. By the end of the story, he has become the crime boss while alienating the woman he loves. Without Michael's love interest, a woman entirely unfamiliar with, and horrified by, this mob world, and his devotion to his beloved father, it would merely be a story of a kid who rises through the ranks of a mob family. By exploring characters that generate the most conflict for each other, our story can build not only in plot but also in meaning as it progresses.

TODAY
Read your outline through the eyes of your ideal reader. Notice how the plot illustrates the theme. As the plot progresses, the story builds in meaning.

Until tomorrow,
Al

DAY 6

"If we go on explaining, we shall cease to understand one another."
— CHARLES MAURICE DE TALLEYRAND

EXPOSITION

Hi Writers,

Sometimes a story can be so overloaded with background information that the reader is drumming his fingers, waiting for the thing to start. There is an art to revealing information. In the opening chapter the reader may need to know that the protagonist was abandoned by his parents, but he may not need to know how, when, or why. Particularly in the beginning of our story, we must focus on writing sharp, distinct details, which are powerful enough to relay the essence of a situation. Our reader has an imagination. The challenge is to strike a balance between providing enough information so that the reader is not lost but not so much that the reader is bored.

Indicating an approaching story point spoils the fun. We want to propel our story forward through conflict, even as we reveal expository information.

TODAY
Search for any material that is not crucial to the set up of your story. Start a separate file called *extra material* and place it here. Later, if you see a spot where this material belongs, place it there.

Until tomorrow,
Al

DAY 7

"We must be willing to let go of the life we have planned, so as to accept the life that is waiting for us." —JOSEPH CAMPBELL

SHOULD I CONTINUE?

Hi Writers,

Today we complete our outline. If we find ourselves in a panic, beset by the fear that we do not really have a story, or that the words are dead on the page, or that it is simply nowhere near where we want it to be – then we need to ask ourselves a few questions, and make a choice.

First, we need to ask ourselves why we wrote this. Then, we need to ask ourselves if these reasons are still compelling, and if it is worth continuing.

Of course the story is not where it needs to be at this point, but what really matters is whether or not it will maintain our interest over these next few months. Only we can answer this for ourselves.

And once we decide, we must commit.

Do we want to stop because we are bored, or because we are scared? Being scared is inevitable. We want assurances. We want to know that we are not wasting our time. Frankly, we would not be artists if we did not fear the result. Sometimes we may not want to continue, but our story has other plans for us.

Sometimes our story is inviting us to see things in a new way.

Many first-time novelists write their coming-of-age story, or *bildungsroman*. Coming of age does not mean becoming a man or a woman in the traditional sense. The dark night of the soul in a coming-of-age story can feel like the death of our truest selves, but it is not. It is the death of our youth, the death of a childish expectation of how we believe things *ought to be*. It is crucial for the writer to make the shift from the personal to the universal, and become more interested in the *nature* of the situation than what he *perceives* it to be. It is from this place of surrendering the result that we might measure whether or not we wish to continue.

This is not necessarily a pleasant experience. When we wake up, we are sometimes confronted by a world that does not operate the way we would wish. It is at this point that we are presented with a choice. We can rail against the injustices done to us. We can stomp our feet and retreat into the endless myriad survival strategies that sustained our hero in Act Two: force of will, manipulation, pleading and bargaining, hoping against hope, dishonesty, self-sabotage, blaming, playing along, closing our hearts and not trusting...

Or we can make a new choice and accept the world as it is. It is from this perspective, when we are more interested in our nature than in our problems that we see our situation as an opportunity to reframe what we thought the problem was, and perhaps even have a sense of humor about the reality of our situation. It is through this experience that we are transformed, that our world is altered, and what we had once hoped for but had seemed impossible now has a chance to live.

Shame is an inevitable part of this process. It is something we must shed, rather than solve. It cannot be solved because it is a double bind. The writer sets out to tell a story about a character who overcomes an obstacle, only to realize that the obstacle still lives within him. "Who the hell do I think I am to write this?" he wonders. "I haven't overcome anything."

He feels like a fraud. Each insight provides further evidence that he has not yet arrived at a solution to his problem. And if he is resourceful, he might tell himself that he just needs to try harder, hack away at his story for another couple of weeks, or months, or decades, to be sure that he is fundamentally unqualified to tell his story – when the truth is that there was nothing to overcome!

Our protagonist does not overcome reality. He accepts the reality of his situation, and in doing so he begins to see his situation in a new way. All stories are, at heart, existential, in that the hero needs to meet himself. He needs to become connected to his true self, that place that is primal, free of expectations, free of belonging to a tribe. It is only from this place that he can make choices that do not create obstacles for him.

When we are connected to our true nature, we operate from a place of understanding, and we are not so susceptible to the patterns and beliefs that had ruled us previously. Our culture does not support creative endeavors. A creative act is an act of courage. Our creativity can be threatening to others, and so, naturally, once we have embarked on this path, it is easy to become riddled with shame and self-doubt for daring to try. How the hell do we know if what we have to say is right or valid or true? But this is not our business. Our business is to speak our truth *in spite* of our doubt, and to move forward *in spite* of our fear. These obstacles are an inevitable part of the process and when they arise, we are presented with a choice. We can either succumb, or we can become curious and investigate the experience.

TODAY
Ask yourself if you are going to continue with your project or put it aside and begin something new. If you decide to continue, commit fully to the work, set a deadline for the completion of a readable draft (83 more days?) and stick to your schedule.

Until tomorrow,
Al

WEEK TWO

BEGINNING/DILEMMA/ INCITING INCIDENT

Armed with a new and more specific outline, we can now begin rewriting the opening to our novel. This week we are addressing the material from our first sentence to the Inciting Incident. As each book length is different, let's divide our total page count by twelve. If our book is two-hundred and forty pages, then we will be working on roughly the first twenty pages this week, or three pages a day.

The opening of our book sets up everything that follows. Although it may appear that it could begin in a hundred different ways, by asking ourselves some questions, we will start to gain clarity on the most effective opening. The key word to remember is *tension*. Let's consider the opening line of Ha Jin's novel *Waiting*. It begins, "Every summer Lin Kong returned to Goose Village to divorce his wife, Shuyu." In this opening sentence he introduces the reader to his protagonist, tells us the man's driving goal, infers a cultural conundrum, and sets up a situation that seeks resolution. Immediate tension. The reader has been presented with a charged situation which seeks resolution. We must continue reading if we are to find out how Lin Kong will achieve his goal. In F. Scott's Fitzgerald's *The Beautiful and Damned*, he opens the novel with many pages of exposition, as if he is bringing us up to date on the goings on in 1920s New York, while at the same time setting up a sense of impending doom.

As our book opens, we are not just setting up the action to follow, but we are also providing context for that action. Our plot is in service to our theme. The action is taking place for a reason. It exists in order to reveal a universal truth such as "crime doesn't pay" or "pride comes before a fall" or "the truth sets us free." Our theme is explored through conflict, and this conflict is revealed through the protagonist's dilemma.

Early in our story, we may notice that our protagonist is struggling. By exploring our protagonist's desire, we are taken directly to the nature of her struggle. For example, in *The Lovely Bones*, Susie has a crush on a boy. She wants to kiss him, and dreams of falling in love, but these dreams are dashed before she has a chance to realize them. Through the story, the desire to return to Earth and experience love is in conflict with the need to accept the reality of her situation, i.e. to move on. Although the dilemma is personal to our protagonist, it is universally relatable. Everyone can understand the desire to hold on to the past, even as it prevents us from moving forward in our lives, or, in this case, Susie's afterlife.

We might be wondering what to do if our protagonist does not appear until later in the story. This is often the case in historical fiction and in stories that span generations, like Jeffrey Eugenides' *Middlesex*. Regardless, we will notice that the dilemma is alive in all of our characters from the beginning. They all have a relationship to the dilemma as it relates directly to our theme.

Lastly, do not intellectualize these questions. We do not need to *figure all this out!* It is more important to inquire than to have the answer. The answers will likely be revealed over time. By exploring the dilemma, we move in the direction of conflict, and it is through conflict that our work becomes more specific.

Notice how most stories begin with the question "Why is this day unlike any other?" This does not mean that the question is answered on page one but that everything preceding this Inciting Incident is in service to it. Alice Sebold's *The Lovely Bones* begins with

Susie Salmon's rape and murder. J.K. Rowling's *Harry Potter and the Sorcerer's Stone* begins with Harry discovering that he is a wizard. Everything that precedes Susie's murder and Harry's discovery exists in order to provide context for these moments. It is not the moment in and of itself that is compelling, but rather the meaning ascribed to it. In the context of the story, what does it *mean* that Susie is killed, or that Harry discovers he is a wizard?

The Inciting Incident is the next story point following the establishment of our dilemma. In Russell Banks' novel, *The Sweet Hereafter*, the Inciting Incident occurs when a school bus crashes through an icy lake in a small Upstate New York town. Ostensibly, it is a story of a town dealing with the aftermath of tragedy, but thematically, it is about the cost of hiding the darkest aspects of ourselves. The bus accident is a catalyst through which the dilemma of holding onto secrets is explored.

In our first draft we may have had a sense of our Inciting Incident, but in the rewrite we are going to use all of our tools to illustrate to our reader precisely why this day is unlike any other. Our secondary goal is to notice how our Inciting Incident is directly linked to the protagonist's dilemma that was set up earlier.

If we sense that some part of our story is not working, we may discover that our characters are veering away from the central conflict. If a scene's conflict is not germane to the theme, it is superfluous. The sneaky thing is that in our first act we are setting up our story, therefore it is not always easy to see until later where our story has gone off the rails. The solution is to continually track it back to the central dilemma, as this will keep us connected to our theme.

QUESTIONS FOR THE WEEK:

1. What is the dilemma at the heart of my story?

2. How can I show the dilemma through my characters' actions?

3. Is the dilemma universal? Is it something with which every character in the story can relate?

4. Is the dilemma primal? Are the stakes high enough to carry the ensuing drama?

5. Do I see the connection between the dilemma and the theme that I'm exploring?

6. What is my protagonist's false belief in the beginning of the story?

7. In the Inciting Incident or "Why is this day unlike any other?" moment, do I see a connection between this moment and my protagonist's dilemma?

8. Is everything in the opening of my story leading to the Inciting Incident?

9. Is there information that the reader still needs to know in order for the Inciting Incident to have its fullest impact?

10. Is there unnecessary information that impedes the narrative drive?

DAY 8

*"A novel's whole pattern is rarely apparent at the out-
set of writing or even at the end; that is when the
writer finds out what a novel is about and the job
becomes one of understanding and deepening, or
sharpening what is already written. That is, finding
the theme."*   —**DIANE JOHNSON**

BEGINNING

Hi Writers,

Where do our story ideas come from? From where do our characters emerge? The process of story creation is mysterious. Our stories are born out of an impulse to make order from chaos.

Stories reveal a transformation, a new way of seeing things. Notice how we dream in archetypes. Our dreams are filled with primal
forces: the killer, the nurturer, the lover, the wise old man, the mysterious stranger, the innocent. It is through these primal forces that
our subconscious seeks to make meaning of our lives and to resolve
seemingly intractable problems.

Our characters are functions of this search. They exist as a
means of illustrating the journey from fear to love, from revenge to
forgiveness, from ignorance to wisdom. The writer's job is to track
this journey in a truthful and compelling way that leads to a transformation.

There is a difference between plot and theme. Plot is *what happens*, while theme conveys our story's underlying meaning. In a wholly satisfying story our theme is in service to the plot and not the other way around.

Clarifying a theme is like staring into the sun. Looking at it head on blinds us to what we are seeking. If we try to figure it out, we become lost in our idea of the story. If I think my theme is "the truth sets us free," that is terrific, but it is also a broad canvas. If I intellectualize this theme I might end up ruining perfectly fine scenes by killing the conflict in pursuit of my idea of this theme.

Our job is not to figure out our story, but to inquire. We are not seeking an answer, but rather, a wider understanding. When we try to figure it out, our story risks becoming ponderous and pedantic.

WHAT IS MY FIRST LINE?

There are an infinite number of approaches to writing a first line. Some authors lead with their voice, while others introduce character, conflict, theme, or just flat out state the premise. In Jane Austen's *Pride and Prejudice*, the story begins with the line "It is a truth universally acknowledged, that a single man in possession of a good fortune, must be in want of a wife." In this statement the author arouses our curiosity by introducing a number of the elements to follow. We know that this story will likely involve the courting habits of the privileged.

In Grace Krilanovich's novel, *The Orange Eats Creeps*, she opens with the line "Dislodged from family and self-knowledge, and knowledge of your origins you become free in the most sinister way." This line is filled with tension from its use of the word *dislodge* to suggest disconnection from self and loved-ones, to the end of the sentence *free in the most sinister way*, suggesting that our genealogy and dependency on loved ones is the tenuous anchor to our moral compass. That the line addresses the reader directly is subtly confrontational and jarringly intimate.

In Allison Burnett's darkly comic novel, *Death By Sunshine*, the narrator B.K. Troop is established in the opening line: "When, after a trial of long months, I had at last finished writing my second novel, *The House Beautiful,* I set down my ballpoint pen and lifted a flute of congratulatory champagne to the mantel mirror." In one sentence the author establishes the character. We know that B.K. is a writer, a romantic, and hilariously self-absorbed.

There are no rules to an opening line, except that it demands we continue reading.

To try to figure out an opening line is too much pressure to place on ourselves. Rather, when we allow our focus to be on the story as a whole, our opening line tends to find us. Although we are moving through our rewrite in a modular fashion, if we insist on nailing the opening line before proceeding, we may become paralyzed by the pressure. In fact, if we feel blocked at any point in the rewrite, it may be that we are not yet armed with the necessary information to write it. Sometimes by gaining clarity on other sections, we discover what the scene is about, and this principle is particularly true of the opening line. If we are pleased with our opening line, that's terrific, and if we are not, we may discover that it is the last line to be rewritten.

SETTING GOALS

Sometimes we set unrealistic goals only to feel defeated when we do not reach them. Rewriting a novel is a marathon, not a sprint. It is important to set small, incremental goals, and move gradually toward them.

This work is more methodical than the soaring heights and occasional deep lows of the first draft. In the long run, we will be more productive if we set realistic goals and do not burn ourselves out on any particular day. Perhaps it is two pages a day – perhaps more, perhaps less. Find a pace that feels manageable over the long run, and use that as a benchmark. Yes, this book is called The 90-Day Rewrite, but if you have written *War and Peace,* you might want to cut yourself some slack.

TODAY
1. Notice where the dilemma lives in the beginning of your story. How can you make it as clear as possible so that the reader understands the nature of your protagonist's struggle?
2. Set a realistic goal for how many pages you will rewrite each day.

Until tomorrow,
Al

DAY 9

"Character, of course, is the heart of fiction. Plot is there to give the characters something to do."

—John Dufresne

CHARACTER SUGGESTS PLOT

Hi Writers,

Our story is far more malleable than we may think. If we feel like the order of events is less than compelling, we can explore other possibilities. (We just make sure that we have a saved copy of the original draft.) We can shuffle our story like a deck of cards. It can be an interesting exercise to explore the infinite number of ways our story can be told. As we play with our story, it will gradually become apparent. We do not need to worry about the areas that still elude us. We work with what we can, and we gradually develop more clarity on the story as a whole.

Some writers have a tendency to graft real life events onto their story, as if a particular incident belongs simply because "that is how it actually happened." Bad reason.

For example, just because a writer has three kids does not mean her heroine must have three kids. If the children are secondary, and we simply need to understand that our hero is a parent, one kid might represent this just fine.

The reader expects each character to exist for a reason. It can be distracting when characters appear purposeless on the page, and we never want to distract from the core dramatic question.

There is nothing wrong with using real life as fodder for fiction. However, it can become problematic when our personal history becomes more important to us than our fictive world. Let's pay close attention to the thematic nature of these events in order to maintain a coherent narrative.

Though we are engaging our intellect through this process, our reason for writing tends to be less conscious. There is something we seek to understand. It is elusive. We must trust the nature of the events rather than the event itself. We must trust our characters more than our plot. Our idea of an event can seduce us away from what the story is actually about. Is *The Great Gatsby* about the struggle to gain respectability? Yes. Is it about obsession and impossible love? Sure. And these primal impulses are important insofar as they inform us of Gatsby's dilemma. What must be resolved in order to gain freedom, and what is his tragic flaw that prevents this? These are the questions that lead to the motor that drives the story.

TODAY
Notice how your characters are a function of the plot. If a character's function is unclear, perhaps he is unnecessary. If a character seems superfluous, consider taking him out, and notice how doing so clarifies the story.

Until tomorrow,
Al

DAY 10

"It is splendid to be a great writer, to put men into the frying pan of your words and make them pop like chestnuts." —GUSTAVE FLAUBERT

TENSION

Hi Writers,

The tension of the characters' dilemma, alive through every moment, carries the story to its conclusion. The dilemma is a universal question, for example, "Will I go along with the group, or be true to myself?" The stakes are life and death. "If I am true to myself, I may be ostracized, but if I go with the group, I may lose myself forever."

The dilemma is a problem that cannot be solved without creating another problem, thus forcing our hero to continually take action until he arrives at a moment of crisis and must surrender his *idea* of what he wants. This surrender allows him to reframe what he wants. As a result of accepting the reality of his situation, he is able to move forward towards the possibility of getting what he wants. He may get it, and it might look nothing like what he thought it would. He may no longer want it at all. Either way, the protagonist has experienced change and achieved growth.

What we feel strongly about is subjective, meaning that it contains within it an opposing argument, though we may not initially be aware of it. Since we are typically drawn to write stories that explore issues we feel strongly about, the more we are willing to investigate the opposing argument, the more specifically we will understand the dilemma. As we imagine the myriad ways that our protagonist and antagonists go about getting what they want, the dilemma becomes clearer.

It is important to note that our idea of our story is never the whole story. For example, we may *perceive* our hero as passive, but even the most passive character has an active inner life, i.e. a dilemma. Our *idea* of passivity may only be the appearance of passive. Our hero must be active or there will never be a shift in perception.

TODAY
By exploring what each character wants in the scene, notice how it offers opportunities to clarify the dilemma.

Until tomorrow,
Al

DAY 11

"The ability to simplify means to eliminate the unnecessary so that the necessary may speak."
—Hans Hoffman

EDITING/MAKING ASSUMPTIONS

Hi Writers,

We do not want to remove words, sentences or passages, unless we know why we are removing them. If we are unsure, we may want to take them out and store them somewhere until we know what to do with them.

Sometimes we write material that excites us, only to reread it later and wonder what it has to do with the story we are telling. It may sound nice or seem interesting, but if it does not make sense or is overly poetic to the point of being obtuse, it does not belong. Every word must be in service to the whole. As we grow as writers we are cultivating a sense of what belongs and what is merely an attempt to impress. When in doubt, simplify. Tell the story and nothing more.

Assumptions in our work lead to writing that is general, confusing, or both. I worked with a memoirist who described blood gushing from a wound as follows: *The blood gushed from my arm like a faucet turned on full blast.*

I asked if that was what it was really like. He said no, and described how the blood squirted rhythmically. He then rewrote the passage, describing the blood as *"gushing from a broken faucet."* However, the example still needed more specificity, because a *broken faucet* could mean many things. Just because his idea of a broken faucet is one that squirts rhythmically does not mean that all readers have the same connotation.

In the final rewrite, it became, *"The blood sputtered from the gash like a faucet on the fritz."*

TODAY
Read each sentence from the point of view of your reader. Notice where you have made assumptions, and where you can be more specific.

Until tomorrow,
Al

DAY 12

"The measure of artistic merit is the length to which a writer is willing to go in following his own compulsions."   —JOHN UPDIKE

MULTITASKING

Hi Writers,

Rewriting a novel involves multitasking. As we rewrite our opening, we are paring down our sentences, reordering scenes, deleting material that does not serve the narrative, dramatizing exposition, and writing the necessary material to make our first act build in meaning as it progresses.

There can be a tendency to fall in love with passages that don't serve our larger story. If we are unwilling to let go of material that is not in service to our story, we are in for a hellacious ride.

Even though we may not be entirely clear, at least consciously, we most certainly have a *sense* of our story otherwise we would not have gotten this far. Something about its very essence has its hooks in us, something that transcends plot. Everything in our story should be in service to this thing.

Just because we like a passage does not mean it belongs. At times, we must be brutal. We need to read the story through the eyes of our ideal reader, asking ourselves if we are being clear, simple, and concise.

Our *desire* to express is the engine that fuels our imagination. The challenge in the rewrite is to remain connected to this primal place. As we rewrite, we are constantly moving between our head and our heart. By holding it loosely, we can better recognize the patterns our subconscious created in the first draft. In the rewrite, we work with these patterns in a way that makes the whole greater than the sum of its parts.

TODAY
Do not settle for the drama of your plot. Practice asking yourself with each sentence that you read, "Why is this happening, and how does it serve the story as a whole?"

Until tomorrow,
Al

DAY 13

"The writer, when he is also an artist, is someone who admits what others don't dare reveal."

—ELIA KAZAN

GETTING MORE SPECIFIC

Hi Writers,

What is the most effective way to unspool our story for the reader? In Act One we are establishing the world and revealing our hero's dilemma. How the dilemma manifests itself will always be connected to that initial impulse. As our story evolves, we begin to reach a sort of critical mass. At this point, we can either turn away from it and succumb to narrative distractions, which on the page can look like a U-turn away from the true drama, or we can continue to investigate the world of our hero's dilemma and diligently follow the thread that so captivated us in its inception.

It takes courage to fully investigate the hero's dilemma. We are exposing ourselves, and this can feel terrifying. There may very well be situations, emotions and experiences that we would rather not explore. But that is what we have signed up for. It is also a narrative gold mine.

I have seen countless writers circle the core dilemma in their stories, paralyzed by their fear of revealing some naked truth. I have done it myself, and probably will again. It is common, but it can lead to procrastination or a vague sort of writing around the real story. At worst, it can lead to abandoning the project.

It is helpful to approach our work as a two-tiered proposition. When we write for ourselves first, and give ourselves full permission to never show it to anyone, our writing tends to be more truthful. It might sound strange, writing something that we cannot imagine putting out into the world, but remember that the purpose of story is to reveal a transformation. When we are willing to write the forbidden, we often arrive at a new understanding of the situation. This wider perspective cannot arise without having examined the darkness and allowed ourselves to expose those naked truths.

Take the risk. You can always delete it later.

When we finish our rewrite, we can decide what we want to do with it. If we have been true to ourselves in the first stage, something magical tends to happen. We experience a shift in perception that we may not have anticipated. We have written the truth, and in doing so, we may discover that we are okay revealing what we have revealed. Those fears that wanted to keep us from writing it have evaporated, or at least they do not have the grip on us that they once did. Those passages that initially felt forbidden may later reveal themselves to be simply a human, poignant part of our story. In allowing ourselves to tell the unadorned truth on the page, our relationship to our story often deepens. If we decide that our story is just for ourselves that is fine too, because the simple act of telling it has given us greater freedom.

TODAY
Find a passage where you sense that you are withholding information. Make a space between each sentence and write two sentences. Keep the new material that makes the work more specific, and delete the rest.

Until tomorrow,
Al

DAY 14

"Prose is architecture, not interior design."
—ERNEST HEMINGWAY

WORDS

Hi Writers,

Our words are in service to our story. Not the other way around. When we get too flashy with our adjectives and adverbs, we may distract and even confuse our reader in ways we might not be aware. We do not ever want to replace substance with style. If every sentence is shouted from the rooftops, important content will get lost in the shuffle.

In painting, a color is understood in relation to another color. A particular green will mean something different depending on the colors with which it is in contrast. Just as darkness can only be understood in relation to light, if every sentence blares to us as a headline, we will have nothing to measure our climax against, and our story will lose its meaning.

If we keep it simple, each nuance will have maximum effect. In the rewrite, we are seeking clarity and meaning.

Stripping our prose to the bone does not mean that we are unconcerned with the rhythm of our sentences. We are interested in the flow of the words insofar as they are in service to our story, and nothing more. If we find ourselves trying to sound clever, or that we are falling in love with our words, it might be time to step back and ask ourselves if we are being clear. Long sentences do not confer genius, nor do big words. In fact, verbosity rarely makes our work more specific, but rather pulls the reader out of the story.

TODAY
Choose a paragraph and just for fun, remove every unnecessary word. Explore how you can condense it to precisely what you wish to say. Once the paragraph shines like a diamond, ask yourself one last question: "Is this paragraph necessary?" If the answer is no, delete the paragraph.

Until tomorrow,
Al

WEEK THREE

OPPOSING ARGUMENT

This week we are rewriting up to the opposing argument, which may occur roughly two-thirds of the way through Act One. The opposing argument is the dilemma seen from its opposite perspective. It is an opportunity to show our readers both sides of the "apparent" problem in order to understand the dilemma. If we were to only show one side it would appear that our protagonist was simply struggling with a problem and we would not fully understand the nature of the conflict.

It is important to note that an opportunity for an opposing argument likely already exists in our manuscripts. Structure is not something that we need to manufacture, but rather it is something that is honed through inquiry.

Story structure should not feel like a math problem. If we ever feel like we are making choices simply to suit our idea of our story's structure, then it is time to stop and explore our protagonist's impulses at this point in the story. By listening to our characters' impulses, we will invariably be led to a more dynamic way to explore the opposing argument.

QUESTIONS FOR THE WEEK

1. Am I dramatizing the dilemma's opposing argument through action?

2. Am I setting up the major characters in my first act?

3. How are my major characters relating to each other?

4. Am I noticing how all of my characters want the same thing?

5. Is there conflict in each scene?

6. Am I noticing how scenes can be reordered, removed, or conflated to heighten the tension and bolster the narrative drive?

7. Is my dialogue alive? Have I fully mined the character's objectives in each scene to maximize the conflict?

DAY 15

"I exhort you also to take part in the great combat, which is the combat of life, and greater than every other earthly conflict."   **—PLATO**

THE ARC OF A SCENE

Hi Writers,

In the rewrite, we seek to make our story as dynamic as possible by exploring the various ways our characters attempt to get what they want. Conflict arises when our characters' attempts are met with obstacles – antagonistic forces that cause them to alter their approach. The back and forth interplay between protagonist and antagonist provides our scene with an arc.

As our work gets more specific in the rewrite, we tend to make discoveries that assist us in making the arc as dynamic as possible. For example, perhaps we have written a scene that begins with a man announcing to his wife that he wants a divorce, and by the end of the scene he is professing undying love. In the rewrite we might explore the specific beats that led him from threatening divorce to proclaiming his true love. Does the man simply turn on a dime? What prompts this reversal? Does he realize that she does not *need* him the way he thought she did? How does he backpedal when he realizes that he has lost her and must win her back? How is their relationship forever altered as a result of him dropping this bomb?

Each scene is informed by the scenes that precede it. By exploring the couple's backstory and all that leads to this particular moment, we arm ourselves with information that informs the scene and make it as dynamic as possible.

We may want to explore these many possibilities through stream-of-consciousness writing in order to discover moments that bring the scene to life. What prompts the man to experience regret, beg forgiveness, rationalize his reason for seeking a divorce, demand an apology, experience doubt, reveal a secret, and suffer a crisis of faith? In short, what are all the ways we can explore the nature of the dilemma through the scene?

TODAY
Notice how your scenes begin and end. Do they build in tension? Does something happen that reveals the characters in a new light? Can you make the scene more dynamic by exploring new ways for your characters to get what they want?

Until tomorrow,
Al

DAY 16

"A writer is, after all, only half his book. The other half is the reader and from the reader the writer learns."   —P.L. TRAVERS

STORY IS A PACT

Hi Writers,

There is a sense of relief in finishing our first draft. We are no longer confronting the blank page when we sit down to do our work.

However, the rewrite process has its own specific challenges in that it engages both our right and left brain simultaneously. We are still actively imagining the world of our story while at the same time wearing our critical hat, editing, tightening loose ends and layering in new information.

One of the challenges of good storytelling is knowing when to reveal information. It is through trial and error that we discover what works best. Removing or reordering a scene can greatly alter the story's meaning. For example, by withholding crucial information we may create an atmosphere of suspense, yet this choice can also affect how our reader understands the story.

In the rewrite we do not want to lose touch with our ideal reader. Story is a dialogue between the author and that reader whose questions we intuitively anticipate by constantly asking ourselves, "Am I revealing character through behavior and action, or am I relying on telling the reader who the characters are?"

Telling something about a character without demonstrating it through behavior will engender suspicion in our reader. I remember, years ago, when I first moved to New York, I had a roommate who was a prodigious blind-dater. She would come home and regale me with her stories. Once she had a lunch date with some guy who midway through the meal reached across the table, took her hand and said, "I just want you to know that you can trust me." She high-tailed it out of there.

As writers, we do not want to be that guy. It is presumptuous to assume that our reader should trust our opinion on anything. We do not want to bury some political screed in our dialogue, or bully our reader into seeing things our way. A story is a pact, and we must hold up our end of the deal. As the writer, we have agreed to simply present the world of our story and allow the reader to have his own experience.

TODAY
1. In removing or reordering scenes, be aware not only of the plot implications, but also of the larger implications to the story, such as tone, pace and meaning.
2. Notice if there is a character that you personally dislike. Have you rigged the story against him, or are you giving him enough rope to hang himself?

Until tomorrow,
Al

DAY 17

"Only trust thyself, and another shall not betray thee."
—WILLIAM PENN

STAYING CONNECTED TO THE SOURCE

Hi Writers,

In the rewrite we are shifting gears between our imagination and our analytical mind. As our story evolves, we begin to see that it is not precisely the book we had imagined. There may be scenes and characters that we thought would be in our first draft, but could not find their way in, while there also may be scenes we cannot bring ourselves to cut, yet they clearly do not belong.

How do we know what to keep and what to discard? How do we make our story become what it is supposed to be? Everything else can be held loosely but that raw primal impulse that got us started is the source of our story. We must stay connected to it as we continue to shed, layer, shift, edit, and add new material.

Through this process we are moving in the direction of the most fully realized version of our story. It is not a linear process, but we do have some guideposts to keep us on the path.

As we move more deeply into our first act, we are looking for ways to show the opposite side of the protagonist's apparent problem. Let's explore how an opposing argument is revealed roughly two-thirds of the way through our first act, thus illustrating the dilemma. In essence, a dilemma is a "damned if I do, damned if I don't" situation. Once we have explored the "damned if I do" through the inciting incident, we must take a look at the "damned if I don't" aspect through the opposing argument. It is through understanding the dilemma that our reader will understand clearly why our protagonist makes his decision at the end of Act One. The opposing argument informs the protagonist's dilemma and keeps our reader connected to our theme.

Let's say a man wants to protect his grandparent's legacy, a sprawling ranch that has been passed down through generations and is now entrusted to him. Times are tough and his ancestors' legacy is in jeopardy. Perhaps, in an attempt to protect the ranch, he commits a crime that puts him in jail. While incarcerated, he realizes that his grandparent's legacy was not their ranch, but rather, their work ethic and integrity. In the end, though defeated, he experiences a shift in perception, and it is from this new understanding that he can build a new life and carry on the true legacy of his forbears.

The dilemma could be that in order to protect his idea of his family's legacy, i.e. the ranch, he must jeopardize his reputation. In the first act it would be important for the writer to understand both sides of the protagonist's dilemma in order to illustrate this for the reader, otherwise the central conflict could become vague and the underlying meaning of the story could be lost. If the inciting incident was a situation that foretold the loss of the ranch and all of the various consequences, i.e. how it might affect his livelihood, his family, his reputation, and his future, the opposing argument might involve the presentation of an alternative, a single nefarious deed that could make all of his troubles go away but flies in the face of who he believes himself to be. Act One is where this dilemma is set up through action, leading inexorably to the decision to commit the crime that sends him into the second act.

Although we may likely have written a scenario that can serve as the opposing argument, the challenge in the rewrite is to make it as clear as possible. If the man lacked integrity, it would weaken the dilemma and confuse the reader. If the man did not care about his family, it would lessen the jeopardy and the reader would not be clear on what was at stake. In the rewrite, we want to look for ways to raise the stakes, not in an attempt to "milk the scene," but rather to clarify the dilemma so that our reader remains connected to the theme.

TODAY
Identify a scenario roughly two-thirds of the way through your first act where an antagonist's actions illustrate the protagonist's dilemma. Explore ways to make this moment emotionally impactful for him.

Until tomorrow,
Al

DAY 18

"Anyone who opposes a pivotal character necessarily becomes the opponent or antagonist. The antagonist is the one who holds back the ruthlessly onrushing protagonist."   **—LAJOS EGRI**

ANTAGONISTS

Hi Writers,

There is a common misconception that our antagonists are the bad guys. This is not necessarily so. In Lajos Egri's classic book *The Art of Dramatic Writing*, his description of antagonists (see quote above) is particularly well worded. Mr. Egri makes a point of describing the protagonist as *ruthlessly onrushing*, suggesting that just as our antagonists want something, so does our hero. As writers, we cannot afford to make value judgments on our characters, otherwise it appears that we are pushing an agenda rather than allowing the reader to become lost in the story. Although the book jacket might suggest otherwise, story is not about good and bad but about cause and effect.

Although an antagonist may be a "bad guy" or a villain, that is not a helpful way to approach it as a writer. An antagonist is just someone who stands in the way of the protagonist achieving his goal. Period. Whatever that looks like.

For instance, in the play *Whose Life Is It Anyway?* the protagonist,

Ken Harrison, is injured in a car accident, leaving him quadriplegic. He was a sculptor, and now without an ability to create, is utterly bereft. The doctors and nurses, friends and family, namely everyone who wants him to live, become his antagonists as he fights for his right to die.

It is helpful to note that once we distill our protagonist's desire to its nature, we see that all of the antagonists in our story want precisely the same thing that he does. This is necessarily so, because our characters' wants are all related to our theme. It is not that Ken wants to die. He doesn't. He wants to live. It is just that he cannot imagine living without the ability to do what he loves. The theme of what it means to live and how we ought to be able to make that choice for ourselves is the question that is explored through the scenario.

If Ken was not a vibrant personality in the beginning of the play who embraced life and cherished his ability to create, his wish to die would be vague and possibly misinterpreted. Similarly, if the antagonists in the story were indifferent to his request, there would be little conflict, and the theme would be unclear.

By recognizing a similarity in the nature of our protagonist and antagonists' desires, we are able to explore ways to dramatize the conflict.

TODAY

1. Track your protagonist's motive through each scene of your first act. Do you see an overarching want that compels her from the very beginning of the act to the end?
2. Notice where the nature of this want is alive for every character in your story.

Until tomorrow,
Al

DAY 19

*"An essential element for good writing is a good ear.
One must listen to the sound of one's own prose."*
—**BARBARA TUCHMAN**

READ IT OUT LOUD

Hi Writers,

A good storyteller is a good listener.

When we tell someone a story, we are listening to that person's response so that we can make adjustments, embellish, clarify and edit. It is a natural process of right and left brain working in concert. Because it is happening so quickly, we may not consciously wonder if our protagonist is likeable or if we have worthy antagonists – but instinctively all of this information is being processed.

It is helpful to read our work out loud. This helps us separate ourselves from our work and inhabit the role of our ideal reader, hearing the rhythm and pacing of our words. It is tempting to fall in love with our prose, but when we hear it out loud (and particularly when we read our work in public), we tend to be more ruthless in our editing. From my years as a stand-up comic, I learned to reduce my words to only what was essential. Anything extraneous killed the joke.

If we sense that something needs to be cut, it probably does. If we are unsure, we can remove it and see if we have lost some essential meaning. Verbosity can produce confusion. By trimming our prose, we often begin to understand our story in a more specific way.

Do not be afraid to trim material that seems unclear or feels like a placeholder for something more specific. By doing this, you are making room for the material that ultimately belongs in the story.

TODAY
Read your work out loud – not just the dialogue, but also the prose. Are you saying precisely what you meant to say? Are there areas that require clarification?

Until tomorrow,
Al

DAY 20

"Fiction reveals truth that reality obscures."
—RALPH WALDO EMERSON

BUT THAT IS WHAT REALLY HAPPENED

Hi Writers,

In writing fiction we inevitably come to that moment that is lifted directly from our real life. Fidelity to real life events can create a block in the rewrite. In an attempt to be faithful to the event, we can lose our connection to the *truth* of our story. The facts of the event are not enough – we must also provide our reader with context; what does this event mean in terms of the larger story? Sometimes we can have such an entrenched *idea* about what happened that we miss the essence of the incident. Our perception of the event can often limit our understanding of the event.

The question to ask is, "What do I want to express through this event?" Seemingly important points become suddenly irrelevant when we explore the nature of the event. It does not matter that our *real* Aunt Maddy and Uncle Petey live in a four-story Coney Island walkup, when what we are interested in is the big fight they had on a Ferris wheel when she admitted the truth that he was not her first love. If it serves our story to be set on the plains of Nebraska, and what we are really interested in is exploring the prickly relationship between the fictional versions of our Aunt Maddy and Uncle Petey, we can still show their fight, though it may take place on a Ferris wheel overlooking a fairground instead of the ocean.

If we try to shoehorn real life events into our fictive world, it will almost certainly throw our story off the rails. It is like when we download a file on our computer and it asks us to put it in a different format to make it readable. By distilling the event to its essence, our reader can be made to understand the nature of Aunt Maddy and Uncle Petey's marriage, regardless of where our story is set.

A similar principle applies to memoir writing. Just because something happened in our life does not mean it necessarily deserves to be in the memoir. If we were to recount every blessed event that happened in our life, the story would never end. If the same beat is played throughout the story, we might want to choose one or two beats to illustrate the point so that our reader does not endure endless repetition. *What happens* is less important than *why it happens.*

TODAY
Notice where you have culled material from your real life and placed it in your fictive world. Wherever an aspect of your real life situation does not satisfy the purposes of your fiction, alter the event. Dressing our fiction with real life situations is like buying a suit off the rack. It is going to require alterations.

Until tomorrow,
Al

DAY 21

"The moment we want to believe something, we suddenly see all the arguments for it, and become blind to the arguments against it.

—GEORGE BERNARD SHAW

OPPOSING ARGUMENT

Every story is essentially an argument that relates directly to the dilemma. Remember that a dilemma is a combination of a powerful desire wedded to a false belief.

In Suzanne Collin's *The Hunger Games*, the author presents a dystopian universe where each day is a desperate struggle to survive, and according to the protagonist Katniss, love does not exist. The story begins with a lottery in which two children from each province are selected to participate in the Hunger Games, a competition to the death. Katniss watches as her younger sister is selected for this Darwinian nightmare, and because this means certain death for the young girl, Katniss bravely volunteers to replace her.

When the boy, Peeta, is selected, we understand that he has been in love with Katniss all of his life, and suddenly the story's central dilemma becomes apparent: "Can love trump survival?"

It is important to note that the theme of our story informs the plot but that plot and theme are separate from each other. The theme (does love trump survival?) is the throughline. The plot is simply the events that arise to reveal the theme in all of its manifestations.

Naturally, these children are thrust into a dystopian world. What better environment to explore the question of love versus survival? If true love can exist in the world of the Hunger Games, then certainly it can exist anywhere. The Hunger Games are a metaphor for the worst part of ourselves. These games are played out for the citizens of the Capital, a bloodthirsty yet overly sentimental mob whose only desire is to have their senses pricked.

Through this journey, Katniss struggles with the question, "Is Peeta's love true or is it a ruse?"

The inciting incident raises the question of true love – this is done through showing and not telling. The act of replacing her sister shows us that it does exist. But now we must explore the opposing argument: "Will Peeta sacrifice his life so that Katniss can live? Just how quixotic is this kid?"

Exploring the opposing argument does not imply some *formulaic* relationship to structure. In fact, it is not even about story. It is a valuable tool in developing a more specific relationship to our theme, whether we are writing a poem, essay, memoir, or theater piece.

The opposing argument is important because it gives the reader a visceral understanding of the dilemma. This understanding is vital, because without it, the reader will not understand specifically what is at stake.

Every plot point is built upon the previous plot point. Without a clear sense of the opposing argument, the tension (or reluctance) surrounding the protagonist's decision at the end of Act One may not be clear.

Whether we are writing a richly nuanced human drama or straight-ahead genre fiction, the principle of opposing argument still holds true. Do not fret that you might not have an opposing argument in your story. You do! It is not a matter of getting this right – it is a matter of developing the most specific relationship to it so that what you are saying rings like a bell. The opposing argument is not something to be figured out. There is a rigor to this work, but it is not strictly a left-brain rigor.

TODAY

If you are struggling to identify the opposing argument in your story, reread the section on dilemma near the beginning of this book. Then choose a scene that is roughly two-thirds of the way through Act One and notice where an antagonist takes an action that forces your protagonist to respond.

Until tomorrow,

Al

WEEK FOUR:

THE HERO MAKES A DECISION

This week we are rewriting to the end of Act One where our protagonist makes an irreversible decision. Notice where there might be a moment of *reluctance* that precedes this decision. Even though our protagonist makes a decision that propels him into the world of Act Two, the reluctance that precedes this decision is crucial to clarify for the reader precisely what is at stake.

The decision is irrelevant if our reader does not understand its underlying meaning. Even in memoir, it is important never to assume that our reader understands our characters' motives. I once asked a memoirist why she acted a certain way with her father in a particular scene, and she said, "Because he's a jerk." But that does not explain her motive. Unless we provide a context for our characters' behaviors, our reader will be lost. Conversely, it is important not to spell everything out – our reader has an imagination. How can we dramatize the meaning in our work rather than stating it outright? If our writing is replete with editorials, let's explore ways to show and not tell by putting our characters into conflict.

Human beings typically do not like change, and this decision is all about change. Our protagonist is embarking on a journey, even if that journey is within. The unknown can manifest itself in an infinite number of ways: a move, a new relationship, or a big promotion. It could mean revealing a secret or even remaining silent. As with all of the story points, the event in and of itself is less important than the *meaning* ascribed to it. In *Crime and Punishment*, what does it mean that Raskolnikov commits murder? Without showing his reluctance or hesitation to commit the act, we do not understand his dilemma. In our first draft we may have been only mildly aware of what was driving our protagonist, but in the rewrite we are being invited to become conscious of these motives.

QUESTIONS FOR THE WEEK

1. Is my protagonist's decision at the end of Act One as dynamic as it can be?

2. What does it mean that he makes this decision?

3. Is the meaning clear to the reader?

4. Is the decision conveyed through action and conflict?

5. Is it clear that this decision is related to the dilemma?

6. Is there a moment of reluctance for the protagonist that precedes this decision?

DAY 22

*"I rewrote the ending of A Farewell to Arms, the last
page of it, thirty-nine times before I was satisfied."*
—ERNEST HEMINGWAY

EXPANDING AND CONTRACTING

Hi Writers,

In the rewrite we are always looking for ways to clarify, tighten, layer information, and reorder or conflate scenes. Our manuscript is a living document; it contracts and expands as we move toward a more specific understanding of our story. There likely are scenes that seem disconnected from each other. Exploring the connective tissue requires imagination. How do our characters get from here to there? As outlandish as our hero's choices may appear, our only job is to support them. In finding ways to support their choices, character is revealed.

Sometimes our first draft is so overwritten that until we boil a scene down to what is essential, we do not know what it is about. It can be challenging to shed writing that we like in order for the truth to emerge. But sometimes it is only by contracting that we understand the scene's raison d'être, and from this place we can write new material that fills out the scene. This is not a scientific process. It involves reading over a scene many times until we notice where the energy and excitement is. The areas that feel lifeless, even if we like the words, is where to start cutting.

We are following our intuition. If we have ever done improvisation, we know that rule number one is to never negate. Our task is to support what our partner has given us and advance the scene. If we suddenly discover that our character is left-handed, we are curious about all that this means. If we discover that he was a spy in the past, we explore how this experience has affected his life in the present. Every choice we make has a ripple effect on the rest of the story.

We do not try to control the world of our story. Our characters will resent us and our imagination will pick up its ball and go home. If we remain true to the world that is being created through us, our story takes on the stink of reality. Our subconscious will make the connections naturally. It is our job simply to be curious about where we are being led.

SETTING UP OUR MAIN CHARACTERS

Most stories tend to set up their main characters in the first act. If we are introducing a major character later in our story, we must have a strong reason for doing so. The first note I got from my editor on my novel, *Diamond Dogs,* was about exploring how to introduce the FBI agent earlier in the story, as he showed up near the middle of Act Two. I did not see how it was possible, but what I did was I foreshadowed his appearance by having him mentioned early in the first act. Even though he was not physically present, the knowledge of his existence heightened the tension and foreshadowed his involvement.

TODAY
Choose a scene that feels overwritten and read it over three times. Notice the difference between "liking the writing" and feeling involved in the world of the story. Strip the scene of all that does not feel alive and utterly necessary. Do it quickly, without thinking too much. Now read over the scene and notice how it speaks to you. Does it have a different feel? Has the meaning of the scene altered? Do the characters seem different? If the scene works as it is, leave it alone. If it requires embellishment, add the details that beg to be written.

Until tomorrow,
Al

DAY 23

"The wastepaper basket is the writer's best friend."
—ISAAC BASHEVIS SINGER

EXPLORING BLIND ALLEYS

Hi Writers,

The rewrite is a re-visioning of our work. We return to the original idea at the heart of our story and ask ourselves how we are exploring it through each chapter.

We listen. We never negate. If an idea comes to us, we explore it. The fear may be that our story will collapse, but what often happens is that we begin to see our tale in a more dynamic way. It is overwhelming to explore new avenues when we already have an entire draft at our fingertips. It is tempting to feel loyal to the work we have done in our first draft, but if we continue to trust our impulses, a new perspective may reveal itself. The story becomes richer, and oftentimes a problem is solved in a way we had not imagined. Storytelling is often counterintuitive. We are thinking outside the box.

TODAY

Find an area that is not quite working and notice where you have made assumptions about your characters. Until you have explored the possibility of your characters making different choices, you cannot assume that their current choices are best. If the scene is not working, you will likely discover that you are holding onto an idea of who your characters are.

Until tomorrow,
Al

DAY 24

"For the things we have to learn before we can do them, we learn by doing them."   —ARISTOTLE

MAKE IT ACTIVE

Hi Writers,

We want to engage our reader emotionally as well as intellectually. Rather than describing what the character experienced, let's find a way to dramatize it. Emotionally riveting work is visceral. Being told that the truth sets us free leaves us unmoved, but the dramatization of that theme in the hands of a master storyteller can be life altering.

Writers who resist transformation often hide behind language. Florid prose becomes a disguise for a writer's uncertainty or lack of content. Verbosity is just empty calories. We must be clear, direct, and take responsibility for what we are trying to say.

There are cues that can clue us in when we are not connected to our story. We will tend to use the inactive verb *is* to string prepositional phrases together. This can be an indication that we have lost touch with the narrative. Too many prepositional phrases will kill a sentence. Read a single page of your work and circle every form of the verb "to be" ("is" "was" "will be" "seems to be" "have been") and every prepositional phrase. Strike them out and notice how the sentence becomes active.

Notice the difference between these two passages:

"Bob was going downtown on the bus to meet George. He knew the bus was going to be crowded, and it was. He was standing across from Sally who was sitting with a parrot on her lap."

Let's look at the same passage, but with active verbs.

"Bob rode the crowded bus downtown to meet George. He stood across from Sally, who sat with a parrot on her lap."

The second passage is more immediate. Although both passages are in the past tense, the latter pulls us into the moment. Do we need the middle sentence, where he knew the bus was going to be crowded, and it was? Depends. If it feels somehow essential to Bob's character, you might want to keep it. Otherwise, it is first draft stuff.

I am not suggesting we remove every *is* verb from our work, but let's be conscious of long sentences that are strung together by this verb. An active sentence creates urgency, and urgency enlivens a narrative.

TODAY
Look for ways to make your sentences active by removing as many *is* verbs as possible.

Until tomorrow,
Al

DAY 25

"None of Misery's details and incidents proceeded from plot; they were organic, each arising naturally from the initial situation."   —**STEPHEN KING**

SOLVING STORY PROBLEMS

Hi Writers,

Sometimes we lose objectivity when we have lived with our story for a while. We see the story through a particular lens, and it is difficult to see it from a new perspective. If we approach our story like it is a giant machine with a million moving parts, we will become overwhelmed. But when we recognize that our story lives fully and completely within us, we connect to the source and it is impossible to make a mistake. The process becomes one of moving inexorably toward the most fully realized version of our story.

We do not have to worry about our story falling apart. This is probably the single greatest fear that prevents writers from solving problems. We tighten up, wanting desperately to hold onto our story, and in doing so we lose connection to our theme. Every problem is an opportunity to make our work more specific.

Most story problems do not get solved in a linear way. As we inquire into the nature of our characters, new possibilities are revealed and the problems resolve themselves.

TODAY
In solving a story problem, connect to what your characters want in a particular scene, even if it seems at odds with the direction that you think your story ought to go. You may discover that in exploring the opposite direction, you will arrive at a more fully realized version of the scene.

Until tomorrow,
Al

DAY 26

"The vampires have always been metaphors for me. They've always been vehicles through which I can express things I have felt very, very deeply."

—ANNE RICE

METAPHOR

Hi Writers,

A metaphor is something that stands for something else. We dream in metaphor. It is the language of our subconscious. The use of metaphor creates a universal emotional experience for our readers. If what is happening in the scene is simply what is happening, we may want to inquire more deeply.

Cormac McCarthy's *The Road* explores a post-apocalyptic world where a father and son travel by foot in search of a respite from the hopelessness of a scorched planet. The world of this story is universal – not that we are facing impending nuclear annihilation, but rather, that we all must face our end. The nuclear winter is a metaphor for our own mortality, for the existential despair one experiences as he begins to slip from this world. A sense of impending doom occupies this novel, a sense of lives at the very end of life. The rendering of this world conveys the universal struggle to hold on against the inevitability of death.

The narrator of Denis Johnson's *Jesus' Son* is a nameless drug addict. As desperate and crazed as he is, the protagonist's dilemma – his addiction – is a universal one. His craving is a metaphor for the unquenchable desire to connect that we all feel.

Metaphor helps us to say a lot in a few words. It enriches the emotional resonance of our story, and subtly brings underlying themes to the forefront. It allows us to make connections between disparate elements in our story in order to reveal deeper truths.

TODAY
Identify a primary metaphor in your story. Notice the myriad ways that your subconscious utilized this metaphor to illustrate the theme. See how brilliant you are!

How can you work with this metaphor to make your story clearer and more dynamic?

Until tomorrow,
Al

DAY 27

*"Whoever knows he is deep, strives for clarity; who-
ever would like to appear deep to the crowd, strives
for obscurity. For the crowd considers anything deep
if only it cannot see to the bottom of the water."*
— **FREDERICK NIETZSCHE**

CLARITY

Hi Writers,

As we approach the end of Act One, we want to be clear on our protagonist's decision that propels him into Act Two. It is not the decision itself that resonates for the reader, but the meaning ascribed
to this event. Notice the reluctance that precedes this decision. The
reluctance keeps our reader connected to the dilemma.

To inquire into the *nature* of the dilemma is different than exploring the *nature* of our neuroses. We have a goal. When we fear
that inquiring into a certain area might collapse our story, this is
where we must plunge.

The fear may be that if we are endlessly curious we will never
complete this draft, that our book will go on forever as we circle our
idea of the story. Paradoxically, as we explore the infinite possibilities of our fictional world, we are led to a new resolution.

We must trust that our initial premise is sound. If we do not
fully investigate the hero's reluctance, we will remain stuck in some

idea of his decision and our story will read like we are trying to sell our reader something.

TODAY
What is the protagonist's specific reluctance that precedes his decision? How does this reluctance illustrate his dilemma?

Until tomorrow,
Al

DAY 28

"I never appreciated 'positive heroes' in literature. They are almost always clichés, copies of copies, until the model is exhausted. I prefer perplexity, doubt, uncertainty, not just because it provides a more 'productive' literary raw material, but because that is the way we humans really are."

—JOSE SARAMAGO

AGAINST CLICHÉ

Hi Writers,

Clichés can occur at the level of plot, character and language. The first draft was not about perfecting our prose. We invariably used placeholder phrases to keep the story moving. *It was a dark and stormy night. He ran like a bat out of hell. She looked like a million bucks.* You get the picture. (Did I just say, *"You get the picture?"*)

Clichés meant something once, but through repetition they have lost their impact and have become a sign of lazy writing. Did he really run like a bat out of hell, or did he lumber up the hill, straining for a first glimpse of home? In the rewrite we are slowing the car down to a mile an hour and carefully pointing out precisely what we see.

Complex and nuanced insights will resonate only if they are specific. As we reread our sentences we may notice a tendency to generalize, or dance around what we are trying to say. We cannot assume the reader understands our intention. It has got to be on the page. A sarcastic line of dialogue needs context. Our reader cannot hear our characters voices as they speak, but if we are specific enough, he will feel like he can.

Our focus shifts constantly as we revise multiple aspects of the novel simultaneously. Structurally, we work towards excavating that *clean line* from the opening image to the decision our hero makes that sends him into the extraordinary world of Act Two. We are weeding out sentences that feel lifeless or redundant. We are ridding our manuscripts of flowery unspecific passages that may have convinced us of our genius in the first draft but now feel leaden and pretentious.

I was working on a scene recently and read a line I had written that went, "The rain pounded the pavement, spilling down the hill in waves." It was fine, though a little clichéd with the word "pounded." I thought to myself, what exactly did the water look like as it washed down the hill, and I wrote, "The water spilled down the hill in braided semicircles."

TODAY
Rid your work of clichéd words or phrases. Be precise. Surprise yourself, and make it your own. Use fresh language to describe what you see.

Until tomorrow,
Al

WEEK FIVE

BEGINNING ACT TWO

This week we are rewriting the beginning of Act Two. Our protagonist has entered a new world, and as a result of making a decision that she cannot go back on, she is experiencing the world in a new way.

QUESTIONS FOR THE WEEK:

1. How has the protagonist's world changed at this point in the story?

2. How has her decision at the end of Act One raised the stakes?

3. How has she grown or changed from the beginning of the story?

4. How are my antagonists standing in the way of her getting what she wants?

5. How has her problem altered from the beginning of the story?

DAY 29

"Conflict is the beginning of consciousness."
—M. ESTHER HARDING

CONFLICT

Hi Writers,

A film director once told me that if you put two actors together in a scene without directing them or staging the scene, the conflict would gradually diminish. If the actors were on opposite sides of the set, they would eventually drift toward each other, their voices would grow quieter, matching each other in volume and tone in an attempt to lighten the conflict.

It is human nature to want to resolve (or avoid) conflict. We are pack animals and the urge to belong should never be underestimated. Writers and artists are courageous because our job demands that we offer our dispatches from the fringe. The first time Ibsen's *A Doll's House* was staged, the audience sat silent at the final curtain because they assumed there was more. They could not conceive of a story that ended with a woman walking out on her husband. It was just not done! In writing his groundbreaking play, Ibsen dared to challenge the status quo.

There can be a tendency in the rewrite to tame the wildness of our first draft, to make it palatable – in short, to kill it. The challenge is to clarify our story while preserving the energy of that initial draft. The tendency in the rewrite can be to temper the conflict, to put our hero in *some* conflict, but not enough that we cannot control it. Our fear is that if we do this, our story could fall apart.

When fear arises, it is natural that we want to solve the story problem as quickly as possible. Remember, Einstein said that we cannot solve a problem at the same level of consciousness that created the problem. Simply put, story solutions are rarely linear. The key in solving the problem is to maintain the tension. Our hero wants the tension to be resolved, and sometimes what can happen is that the hero and the author's fear can meet in the back room and strike a deal behind the author's back. We must be willing to follow through to the end with what it is that compels our hero.

Our story is far more malleable than we may think. We must be willing to explore the vast reaches of our character's experience, to allow our *idea* of our story to collapse, so that the real story can live.

TODAY
Follow your characters' impulses. In every scene, notice where you are not allowing your characters to say or do what they wish for fear of the story falling apart. Explore the possibility that they do just that. Trust that they will lead you to the most dynamic and fully realized version of your story.

Until tomorrow,
Al

DAY 30

"It's déjà vu all over again."

—Yogi Berra

BANISH REDUNDANCIES

Hi Writers,

Sometimes we repeat ourselves. This can be really tiresome...really. Redundancies are not only a sign of lazy writing, but they also can pull us out of the story by interrupting the narrative flow.

Redundancies may occur at the level of rehashing story information, harping on the same theme, or using the same word or phrase within close proximity. Some words are like suntan lotion: a little goes a long way. If you are going to use the word *eidolon*, fine, but not on every page.

When we read our work out loud we can catch most of the redundancies and find ways to remove them. Let's try an exercise. Read the following short paragraph, and explore ways to convey the information without being redundant.

"Bob drove to work early. He worked six blocks from home, and when he got tired of working in his office, he did his work from the donut shop next door."

See if you can convey all the information and only use the word *work* once.

"Bob drove six blocks to his office. When he got tired of staring at the same four walls, he worked from the donut shop next door."

Now let's look at a common problem: how to prevent exposition from becoming redundant. For example: a character may need to relay information to someone the reader has already met. How can we explore the second character's reaction at hearing the news, without the reader having to hear it again?

There are as many solutions to story problems as there are curious writers. Perhaps the narrator could tell us that the story was relayed and then show us the other character's response. Or maybe it could be dramatized and the second character could demand to know the story, and we could see the story told again, but from a new perspective, thus revealing new information about the characters' relationships.

Lastly, let's discuss structural redundancy. Sometimes a beat can be played out repeatedly through varying situations, and the redundancy is not at the level of words or situations, but rather, of tension. The story is not building through rising stakes. This may be a structural problem and it can be solved by first recognizing the redundancy. As we approach the end of our first act, let's revisit the act and notice where we can tighten our work by removing beats at the level of plot.

As Ernest Hemingway says, *"Every writer needs a good bullshit detector."* We must be willing to acknowledge when something is not working and have the guts to fix it. We may want to consider tearing out some scenes that *feel* emotionally similar but add little new information.

Fiction is different from real life. Real life has its mundane moments. We eat, we work, we laugh, we cry, we sleep – we do it again. The purpose of fiction is to imbue these events with meaning. We are not interested in the *appearance* of eating and sleeping; we are interested in the underlying meaning that is being expressed through these incidents.

TODAY

Notice your work's redundancies at the level of words, plot and theme, and explore ways to banish them.

Until tomorrow,

Al

DAY 31

*"Imagination is the voice of daring. If there is any-
thing Godlike about God it is that. He dared to
imagine everything."*   —**HENRY MILLER**

VOICE

Hi Writers,

In the rewrite, a voice begins to emerge.

We do not often think about our own voice. Just hearing it out
loud makes us uncomfortable.

"Is *that* what I sound like?"

Then there is our voice on the page. Sometimes we want to
make it sound more impressive. We want to turn up the treble or
give it some reverb. Our naked voice can make us feel, well...ex-
posed. In the rewrite it can be tempting to lose touch with what is
important: trusting that our story is enough.

As we strip down our prose, a clearer voice emerges. It takes
courage to edit writing we liked, even when it obfuscates the meaning of our work. If we are unsure whether a word, sentence or passage belongs, we might consider removing it temporarily to see how
it reads. More often than not, if we are unsure, the cut brings the
passage to life.

I remember reading work my editor had gone through with a
red pen and thinking, "This is so much clearer." It was just a word

here and a word there, but the result was a cleaner line and a clearer voice. To do this for ourselves requires a ruthlessness that we held at bay in the first draft.

TODAY
If you are feeling lost in a power struggle between style and content, fighting to hold onto precious writing that feels at odds with expressing a thought or idea clearly, then you must be ruthless with your red pen.

Until tomorrow,
Al

DAY 32

"Hope begins in the dark, the stubborn hope that if you just show up and try to do the right thing, the dawn will come. You wait and watch and work: you don't give up."   **—ANNE LAMOTT**

SHOWING UP

Hi Writers,

Some of us will complete our rewrite in 90 days. However, each book is different, and every writer works at his own pace. If it is taking you a little longer, you have not fallen behind, and you have not failed.

It took J.D. Salinger ten years to write *Catcher in the Rye*, while William Faulkner wrote *As I Lay Dying*, in six weeks while working in a factory and claims to have not changed a word. Tolstoy took a dozen years to complete *War and Peace*, while Ernest Hemingway wrote *The Sun Also Rises* in three months.

It is easy to get lost in the rewrite, but with a deadline and specific guideposts, that is less likely to happen. There was urgency to writing the first draft. We were in a state of creative frenzy, hurtling towards the end. In the rewrite we return to Earth and the work becomes methodical.

In these 90 days, we are making a second pass through our work and developing a set of tools that allows us to explore our work more specifically. If we are not finished with our first act, that is fine. It is more important that we develop an approach to the rewrite. This is methodical work. It takes reflection and often many passes through the story to get it to where it wants to be.

TODAY
If you're feeling off-target, set a realistic goal for completing your second draft based on your total page count and the average number of pages you have been rewriting in a day. Mark the date on your calendar, and keep going.

Until tomorrow,
Al

DAY 33

"You couldn't get hold of the things you'd done and turn them right again. Such a power might be given to the gods, but it was not given to women and men, and that was probably a good thing. Had it been otherwise, people would probably die of old age still trying to rewrite their teens."   —STEPHEN KING

FEELING STUCK: RULES VERSUS PRINCIPLES

Hi Writers,

Creativity cannot be reduced to a set of rules. There is no such thing as an immutable step-by-step approach to the rewrite process. However, there are principles that when absorbed can help to instill a process.

Yes, there are some basic steps, but sometimes the order gets shuffled, and when we try to quantify a set of rules, we tend to get stuck. The desire to write is the desire to evolve. Every rewrite experience is different. It is a process of inquiring into the essence of something that always feels slightly beyond our reach. When we try to grab onto it, it evades our grasp, but when we hold it loosely, we are led to a deeper understanding of its nature.

If we are feeling stuck, it is helpful to step back and return to basic story principles until we have confidence in what we are trying to say. Reread the section on dilemma and be willing to revisit your outline. Our idea of our story is never the whole story. The rewrite process is a process of shedding our idea of the story for the full story. Stay with it and let the story be more important than the result.

At this stage in the story, we want to explore how our protagonist's decision at the end of the first act has led her into a new world.

TODAY
1. If you are feeling stuck, return to your outline and notice where your story wants to be altered.
2. Notice how your protagonist's decision at the end of Act One has altered the way she is relating to other characters in Act Two.

Until tomorrow,
Al

DAY 34

"If you accept your limitations you go beyond them."
—BRENDAN FRANCIS

ACKNOWLEDGING OUR LIMITATIONS

Hi Writers,

It is inevitable that we confront our limitations through the rewrite process. This is humbling, even scary. We feel lost, like we have taken on more than we can handle. We may wonder what the hell we are trying to say.

On some level, it is true that we are in over our heads, but this is because we are not *supposed* to fully understand our story. We are channels for all of these characters, situations, images and ideas, and through the process of inquiry a coherent narrative is revealed to us.

It is important to understand this process, rather than give in to the desire to make meaning out of our confusion. This process is an act of faith, but it is not an act of blind faith. We have faith in the story within. A mysterious force has been guiding us, and when we trust this, we connect to the aliveness of our story.

By acknowledging our limitations and focusing on the more *technical* aspects of the rewrite – like tightening our prose, clarifying our sentences, banishing clichés and redundancies – our story is revealed to us in a deeper way.

TODAY
Make a list of your strengths and weaknesses as a writer. Do not judge them. Simply notice them. Acknowledging your limitations will lead you to a deeper understanding of your story.

Until tomorrow,
Al

DAY 35

"If you have a good ear for dialogue, you just can't help thinking about the way people talk. You're drawn to it. And the obsessive interest in it forces you to develop it. You almost can't help yourself."

—ROBERT TOWNE

DIALOGUE

Hi Writers,

The surest way to kill the aliveness of our characters is by insisting that they always make sense. When we follow the labyrinth of most conversations, we discover one constant: people are always trying to get what they want. This does not mean that characters are always clear in articulating their desires, or that they are being truthful, or that they must even understand each other.

The purpose of dialogue is to reflect the life and death stakes for our characters. Amidst the most mundane exchange is a yearning for something more. By staying connected to our characters' driving wants, their speech reflects an attempt to achieve these desires. Dialogue is not linear, nor is it logical. With each attempt, our characters are met with antagonistic forces. The tension builds through the scene as each character attempts to realize his goal.

If our prose feels wooden or transparent, as if we are just trying to move the story forward, we can ask ourselves what the characters want. The playwright Harold Pinter wrote elegant human studies that mined the world of the unspoken. At first glance his plays read as banal conversations, but upon further investigation, beneath the thin veneer of civility live tectonic shifts, life and death struggles.

In the rewrite, if a scene is not working, it does not take long to pull out a fresh sheet of paper and write a stream-of-consciousness dialogue. Write it quickly. Surprise yourself with what the characters want to say. It is often in the rewrite that dialogue comes alive. We have a little more security with our structure and we can loosen the reins.

Language is a means of communicating desire. Whether it has to be seen and heard, to gain sympathy, to curry favor, to get information, to feel close, to punish, to win the girl, to hurt, to destroy, to reassure, to secure a position – we speak in an attempt to get something.

But here is the thing: we rarely come out and say what we really want, because within every scene is an antagonistic force. Our characters all have something at stake.

In real life, people rarely say what they think and feel. Why would we expect our characters to do this?

Until we get out of the way, our characters are all going to sound like us.

Great dialogue contains tension. It understands what is at stake, and it walks that line. Great dialogue is specific. A single line can tell us a great deal about a character.

I ran into a friend whom I had not seen in a while.

"How's life?" I asked.

He sighed. "I want a car with a door that opens on the driver's side."

One last thing: Our characters do not have to speak. If they do not want anything, keep them quiet until they tell you their heart's desire.

TODAY
If you have a scene in which the dialogue feels stilted, write a stream-of-consciousness dialogue between the characters for five minutes. Focus on their attempts to get what they want. Do not worry about it making sense. When you have finished it, notice what you can use in your work.

Until tomorrow,
Al

WEEK SIX

OUR HERO EXPERIENCES FALSE HOPE

This week our protagonist will experience something that leads him to believe in the possibility of achieving his goal. This is a crucial point, because without it, the reader will not understand the meaning the protagonist ascribes to his goal.

Each story point is built upon the previous point. Without the protagonist's decision at the end of Act One, there would be no context for this moment of false hope, which then informs the midpoint, and so on. By putting our protagonist in a situation that causes him to believe that he has a shot at achieving his goal, we are glimpsing the power of our hero's will. Oftentimes when we experience a victory, we temporarily forget the underlying struggle that we are actually engaged in. We mistake winning the battle for winning the war. Again, it is the difference between solving a problem and resolving a dilemma; this point in the story is an opportunity to show our reader the meaning our protagonist makes out of his goal, so that when he arrives at the end of Act Two, we will understand what it means for him to reframe his relationship to it.

In Act Two, the gulf between what our protagonist wants and what he needs begins to widen. He began the story with a false belief. He has made meaning out of it, and as the story progresses through Act Two we see, through circumstance, precisely how this false belief influences his choices. The stakes are raised and the conflict heightens as a result of the protagonist attempting to square his goal with his struggle against the antagonistic forces that conspire to have him question this false belief.

QUESTIONS FOR THE WEEK

1. What does this moment of false hope look like for my protagonist?

2. What has he discovered, overcome, or figured out?

3. How can I show an identifiable shift in my protagonist at this point in the story, to illustrate precisely how he has grown or changed from the beginning?

4. How has my protagonist's relationship to the antagonists altered as a result of this temporary victory?

5. How does the moment of false hope illustrate my protagonist's idea of his goal?

6. Can I see how his idea of his goal is going to shift as the story progresses?

DAY 36

"To produce a mighty book, you must choose a mighty theme. No great and enduring volume can ever be written on the flea, though many there be that have tried it."   —HERMAN MELVILLE

PLOT

Hi Writers,

Notice how our protagonist's goal is directly related to her moment of false hope. Oftentimes we begin to see our protagonist's goal more clearly in the rewrite. We might think that our protagonist wants freedom, but upon further inquiry, we may discover that it is really justice that she seeks. There may be a similarity between the two, but as we get more specific with the want, our story becomes clearer.

Our plot does not proceed in a linear fashion. It builds in complication as opposing forces stand in the way of our protagonist achieving his goal. Ultimately, story is an argument that mines a theme, and it is the writer's job to explore both sides of this argument with equal integrity. If we don't, the conflict will seem manufactured. If we demonize our antagonists, there can be no true transformation. The purpose of story is not to promote an agenda; it is to resolve a dilemma through a shift in perception. If the writer is not curious about the outcome, how can we expect our reader to be?

Our idea of the story rarely carries us to the end. We must trust those random impulses that may initially appear at odds with where we think our story ought to go, and be open to opportunities to make our story as dynamic as it wants to be. If we are not holding our story loosely, our writing can become forced.

As our story moves forward, it turns on choices our protagonist makes, choices based on her driving want. This driving want, or desire, never changes through the story, though it may manifest itself in a variety of ways. For example: if a character wants to be loved, he might get engaged in pursuit of this desire, and then he might get married to secure this desire, and later, he might decide that he does not feel loved the way he had expected, and he might choose to get divorced. But his driving want, to be loved, never changes. Our protagonist's desire is the throughline of our story. It might not initially seem like that, but as we continue to inquire, it will gradually reveal itself. This is necessarily so because our protagonist's desire is the vehicle through which our theme is explored.

The key story points in our protagonist's journey are connected to her goal. This is because character suggests plot. Inquiring into the relationship between plot and character can often provide insight into our story. Notice how the dilemma, inciting incident, opposing argument, decision, initial success, temptation, suffering, surrender and battle scene are all connected to this one goal. Continuing to explore this will keep us on course while allowing our story to become as fully realized as possible.

Remember, story structure is not a formula. By inquiring into the connection between our hero's goal and these pivotal moments in our hero's journey, we are finding ways to make our story as dynamic as it can be.

TODAY

1. Notice the relationship between your protagonist's want and the story points. These two elements inform each other.

2. If you're unclear on your protagonist's moment of false hope, be curious about what she wants at this point in the story and search for a way to show the reader how it is within her grasp.

Until tomorrow,
Al

DAY 37

"Have something to say, and say it as clearly as you can. That is the only secret of style."

—MATTHEW ARNOLD

STYLE

Hi Writers,

We can get self-conscious about style. Sometimes we will read a writer we admire and assume that their style was something they created. Our style, the voice through which our story is expressed, develops naturally, and we have very little to do with it, even in the rewrite. When we focus on style we are moving into territory that is more about our idea of people's perception of our writing, and less about what we are trying to say.

James Ellroy's first draft of *L.A. Confidential* was too long, according to his publisher. Apparently Ellroy's agent sat down with a page and knocked out half the words. Upon reading it over, Ellroy realized that none of the story was lost, but suddenly the writing was tight and crisp. Ellory took a machete to his manuscript, and hence, the Ellroy style was born.

Our style is in service to our content. If Dickens wrote in the style of Twain, it would not work...and vice versa. We can ruin our good work by trying to adopt a style. We cannot figure out our voice. Our job is to be a channel for the story to emerge.

TODAY
Your style is something that you have little control over. If you find yourself worrying about your style, or comparing your work to someone you admire and coming up short, this means that you are human.

Until tomorrow,
Al

DAY 38

"Doubt is not a pleasant condition, but certainty is absurd."   —VOLTAIRE

CERTAINTY

Hi Writers,

There is a particular comfort that comes from being certain. We can shut out the world, all of that noise and confusion, and rest in the assurance that we are right. Except that certainty rarely contains the whole story. Certainty is the death of curiosity, and for writers it limits us to our preconceived notions of the way things are.

Let's say we are writing a story from the point of view of a serial killer. This would require us to wonder about the *nature* of a serial killer. It would also require dropping any preconceived ideas about what it would mean to be one. Are serial killers necessarily unkind, antisocial, a constant threat, and so on? If we were to write this story, we would have to accept that he is a human being. How does he think? What does he believe? What does he yearn for? We would need to inquire into where he lives, how he dresses, and how he rationalizes his actions. In short, we would have to *care* about him. Otherwise we would be merely writing our idea of him.

There can be a desire to distance ourselves from antagonistic forces. Real inquiry disrupts certainty, forcing us to confront what we might rather avoid but which may lead us to a clearer and more specific relationship to our story.

Though the serial killer example may be extreme, there are plenty of issues that may cause us to withdraw our curiosity: sexism, bigotry, violence, infidelity, etc. When we inquire into these elements and question our assumptions, we give our story a chance to live.

For those of us writing memoirs, perceptions of our family invariably inform our work. We may hold tightly to our "story," resisting the uncomfortable necessity of approaching it from different angles. Loosening our grip on what we believe allows for a wider perspective. This is not to imply that what we believe is incorrect – it is not. There is just more to the story.

There is a difference between certainty and knowing. A fundamental knowing is like a steady rock beat. It is unwavering. Knowing is the result of persistent inquiry. It contains all paradox. Knowing lives beyond our preconceived idea. It has been road-tested against reality. When one knows, there is no need to argue or defend. Certainty has a white-knuckle quality. It encompasses an unwillingness to hold one's beliefs to the test for fear of the outcome. When we know something to be true, we do not fear being wrong – we are more interested in the nature of *why* it is true.

TODAY
Knowing comes from having clarity on *why* your story ends the way it ends.
1. Examine the ending to your story, where the dilemma is resolved. And then, track your story backwards from the ending to the section where you are stuck.
2. Explore the reasons that this section is essential in leading you to your ending.

Until tomorrow,
Al

DAY 39

"A word is not the same with one writer as with an-
other. One tears it from his guts. The other pulls it
out of his overcoat pocket." —CHARLES PEGUY

TECHNIQUE

Hi Writers,

We have all read that perfect book, the one that immersed us so deeply in its world that we were completely unaware of the author's *technique.* The story gathers force and culminates in a revelation that brings order to all of the preceding chaos, and distills the human experience to something so simple and obvious that we were unable to see it, and when we finish, we are breathless at the author's ability to write with such wisdom and authority.

Is it possible that the author did not set out with this understanding? Perhaps the clarity arose from persistent inquiry rather than one blinding flash of inspiration. Sometimes I think the only difference between the amateur writer and the pro is the depth of their willingness to inquire. Staying curious in the midst of our doubts and fears can be challenging, but when we make the process more important than the result, we are always rewarded with new insight.

As we continue to inquire, we are shedding our preconceived notions for a larger truth, one that contains all of the apparent contradictions in our story.

TODAY
Write down in one sentence what your story is about. Tape this to your computer. Look at it regularly and notice if it continues to hold true. If it doesn't, peel it off and rewrite it.

Until tomorrow,
Al

DAY 40

"The past is prologue."
—WILLIAM SHAKESPEARE

BACKSTORY

Hi Writers,

When we are feeling stuck, it is inevitably because some part of our backstory is unclear. Backstory refers to what happened before our story began and is often revealed through exposition. A clearer understanding of our backstory will inform our characters' present circumstances.

The challenge in clarifying backstory is to resist forcing it to conforming to our idea of the story. A character's place of birth, level of education, relationship history, family dynamic, culture, ethnicity, religious beliefs, and political leanings are all in service to our story. Character is malleable; all of this information is changeable.

The act of seeking the ideal character is not something we can figure out. As we inquire into our story, ideas about our character's past will come to us. They might seem surprising and unusual. They might even appear to want to take our story in a different direction.

Sometimes the appearance of a different direction is really just a stretching of the original idea. Nothing is lost if we entertain an idea for a few moments, yet I am frequently surprised at how rigid new writers can be about this. It is almost as if they are trying to hold the whole story in a small container and fear that to add one more idea might lead to a super-saturation point.

Let's say that I have a character who feels somewhat nebulous. He is a Senator, running for reelection. As I inquire into his backstory, I sense that while married he had a child with another women, a situation that has been kept quiet for years. What on earth does that have to do with my main story about his best friend, a priest who is dying and wrestling with the decision of whether or not to reveal a dark secret?

I begin to wonder if this is a story about secrets. Perhaps I wonder what it means to have a secret, and if it is possible to be forgiven when a secret has been held for such a long time that it has affected the lives of many people. Perhaps I wonder about the value of revealing the truth, and weighing revelation against silence. Perhaps I wonder about integrity. Should a man come clean about his past, even if it means it could adversely affect not only his career, but the lives of his family?

All of these questions sprang from the single impulse: "What if the Senator had a child with another woman?" The nature of "child with another woman" in the context of this story might have to do with *secrets*. In another story, the nature of "child with another woman" might involve issues of responsibility, isolation, guilt or forgiveness. It is valuable to be attuned not only to how new backstory information affects the drama, but also to its deepening of the greater meaning at the heart of our work.

TODAY

Scan your story up to this point and ask yourself the following questions:

1. Is the backstory information that I've included necessary?
2. Does it belong here or can I reveal it later?
3. Can I dramatize the way this information is revealed?
4. Can I *layer in* essential information, thus dropping any unnecessary passages?

Until tomorrow,
Al

DAY 41

"The thing should have plot and character, begin-ning, middle and end. Arouse pity and then have a catharsis. Those were the best principles I was ever taught."   **—ANNE RICE**

THE BALANCE BETWEEN PLOT AND CHARACTER

Hi Writers,

We've heard the terms "plot-driven" and "character-driven." The former tends to mean that little attention is paid to creating fully drawn characters, while the latter tends to mean that very little happens.

Each story has its own pace. Sometimes in attempting to amp up the narrative drive, we can throw our story out of balance by excluding crucial information. As we search for the most effective way to tell our story, and inevitably trim our material, we do not want to discard the essential. We want our story to breathe.

Readers crave specificity of character, but character and plot are inextricably linked. Without conflict between protagonist and antagonists, our story collapses.

If we focus strictly on the plot without having a clear understanding of what is at stake for our characters, the reader will not care. It is a paradox that when plot is in service to character, a story becomes truly immersive.

So, how do we do this? We put ourselves in the position of our ideal reader, that curious soul who asks all the right questions. This happens naturally in the rewrite when we continue asking the overarching question, "What is my story about?" This anchors us to the tension. As we make choices about what to reveal and when to reveal it, over time our story is revealed to us.

TODAY
Are you removing too much from your story in an attempt to quicken the narrative? By simply being aware of the struggle to balance plot and character, you may notice where you are over-editing or under-editing.

Until tomorrow,
Al

DAY 42

"All the ills of mankind, all the tragic misfortunes that fill history books, all the political blunders, all the failures of the great leaders have arisen merely from a lack of skill in dancing."   —MOLIERE

IT'S A DANCE

Hi Writers,

Without the continual pressure of conflict, our story dies. The rewrite is an opportunity to bring our story to life by exploring the moment-by-moment conflict between our protagonist and her antagonists.

It is important to understand that our idea of our characters is necessarily incomplete. In the same way that we will never fully understand ourselves, how can we assume that we truly know our characters? They are inextricably tied to the demands of the dramatic question. Our characters exist somewhere deep within our subconscious, which is why we so often hear writers say, "My characters take on a life of their own."

Every writer wants her characters to spring to life, for the drama to gather force and the story to turn with ever-mounting stakes. It is the storyteller's task to marry the freewheeling right-brain aspect of this process with the more technical rigors of story-structure. When richly drawn characters meet a powerful dramatic question, the result is a compelling narrative.

As we move into rewriting Act Two, we may come across long passages that do not seem to be working. Perhaps we are unsure about how to shape them, or order the events within a passage itself. We might even be confused about our own intentions when we wrote it. Almost inevitably, vast stretches of our first draft prose can feel pedestrian, tedious, overwrought, and just not *right*. We may wonder how we can say it in the way our favorite author would.

The real question to ask ourselves is: "How do I marry the aliveness of my characters to the needs of my story?"

It's a dance.

There are times we may like a scene that we have written even though we are not quite sure how it belongs in the story. This does not necessarily mean that we need to get rid of it. By exploring *why* it belongs, we may discover a new layer to the scene.

There is a gentle give and take in a dance, a constant process of paying attention to our partner's needs as we gently guide them in the right direction. We must guide our characters with the same kind of gentle attention. You may say, "I am not entirely sure where my story should go," and that is fine. It is all a part of the dance.

TODAY

1. If you find yourself saying that your character would not do something, yet the needs of your story are telling you otherwise, consider the possibility that your character might surprise you.

2. As your protagonist achieves a moment of false hope, notice how there is an identifiable shift in him between this point and the beginning of the story.

Until tomorrow,
Al

WEEK SEVEN

THE MIDPOINT:
OUR HERO EXPERIENCES TEMPTATION

This week we are rewriting up to the midpoint of our story. At this point, the protagonist will experience temptation to retreat back to the familiar rather than going forward into the unknown. This temptation is a crucial stage in the story because it often involves a turning point. It is less important to figure out what the midpoint event is than it is to inquire into a moment somewhere in the middle of our story where our protagonist is tempted. It is common for writers to get stuck at this point or for the work to meander. If the story feels flat, or a little boring, we might be holding a little too tightly to our idea of how the story should play out. In revision, the challenge is to remain connected to the characters' impulses while exploring creative ways to raise the stakes. If we can identify the conflict in a scene, we will discover where the dilemma lives. The challenge then becomes exploring the scenario that best exploits this dilemma.

Our ideas are rarely fully formed right out of the gate. It is only through rigorous inquiry that we arrive at the most dynamic version of the scene. Remember that our protagonist's dilemma involves two elements: a powerful desire and a false belief related to this desire. As we explore potential midpoint scenes, notice how these two elements conspire to turn the story in a new direction. If the moment does not feel strong enough, we might be curious about the role that our antagonist plays. On its surface, there is nothing particularly logical about the midpoint because this is where the story often moves in a new direction. It is through the hero's temptation that he commits fully toward achieving his goal.

QUESTIONS FOR THE WEEK

1. What does my protagonist want?

2. What is the false belief or misperception that has been guiding my protagonist through the story?

3. Where in the middle of the story does an event happen that leads to a moment of temptation for my protagonist?

4. How does his choice at this point in the story alter his trajectory?

5. What does this choice mean, and how does it relate specifically to my protagonist's dilemma?

DAY 43

"The difference between reality and fiction? Fiction has to make sense."　　　—TOM CLANCY

TIMELINES

Hi Writers,

Our manuscripts may contain two or more characters whose separate storylines run concurrently. We may discover that our timelines do not quite line up. These logistical problems can strike writers with dread. "My God, my story is ruined," we fear.

A scene in my most recent novel involves one character going on a date, while simultaneously, another character is arrested and briefly thrown in jail. Later that evening, they meet at a diner.

The problem in the first draft was that I wrote the entire date scene *before* he got arrested. After her date, she was dropped off at her hotel, and across the street, the guy from jail was already sitting in the diner, which meant that in the course of her short drive home from her date, he had been arrested, spent hours in jail, and been released. The timeline made no sense. My solution was to have him arrested before her date, and then cut away from the date to show him in jail, and then when she is dropped off at home, there he is, sitting in the diner.

In retrospect it seemed obvious, but it was not, because I had this idea that he had to get arrested late at night when he was sleeping.

However, when I let go of this idea, the problem solved itself. This guy got up at five a.m. and worked like a dog. Why would he not fall into bed when he got home from work? He could be fast asleep at 6:30 when the cops showed up. My fixed idea had prevented me from exploring other possibilities.

It is important to remember that our story is infinitely malleable, and that our characters are simply functions of our theme. Sometimes we can get so fixed on our ideas that we are unwilling to look at our story in a different way.

When we are willing to let go of our idea of a line, a scene, and even what we believe the story is about, we make room for the real story to emerge.

TODAY
Do not assume that because a timeline is off, your story is going to fall apart. Note the essential elements and explore creative ways to realize them.

Until tomorrow,
Al

DAY 44

"A scrupulous writer, in every sentence that he writes, will ask himself at least four questions, thus: 1. What am I trying to say? 2. What words will express it? 3. What image or idiom will make it clearer? 4. Is this image fresh enough to have an effect?"

—GEORGE ORWELL

ASKING THE RIGHT QUESTIONS

Hi Writers,

Remember: this is just our second pass through our story, so let's stop doing a number on ourselves. If we are wringing our hands and inching out on the ledge, perhaps we need a reality check. If we started with the 90-Day Novel, we are less than five months in. Let's ask ourselves the terrific George Orwell questions seen above until they become instinct.

It can be tempting at times to abandon our work, to think it is unimportant and claim to be bored, but this is a setup. Boredom is fear. If we are dragging our butt out of bed and staring at the computer screen in a bloodless stupor, we might need to take an afternoon off and get some fresh air.

When Michelangelo created David, he carved away all of the marble that was not in service to his masterpiece. We trust that our story lives somewhere within this morass of words; it is our job to remain curious as we continue to shape it.

If we are feeling disconnected, we can return to the dramatic questions:

"What is my story about?"
"What am I trying to express?"
"How are my characters a function of the dramatic question?"

These broad questions will bring us back to that original impulse, allowing us to sit down at our desks with a clear mind and a renewed purpose.

TODAY
1. Write for five minutes, beginning with "The truth I'm resisting in my story is…"
2. Notice what comes up and how it leads to a deeper understanding of your story.

Until tomorrow,
Al

DAY 45

"Never mistake motion for action."
—Ernest Hemingway

THE RIGOR OF STORY STRUCTURE

Hi Writers

There is a rigor to story structure. The challenge in trusting our instincts is to not eschew structure in the process. Although we are listening to our impulses, there can be a tendency for the new novel writer to fall in love with every blessed idea. We can become so enamored of our ideas that we cling to them as if they are the last ones we will ever have, sometimes even mashing them all together in a stew as if more ideas means a more interesting story.

It does not.

Ideas are a dime a dozen. Our subconscious cranks them out like child's play. Unless our ideas are filtered through the lens of a unifying theme, their meaning risks being misunderstood or lost. When our story is about a hundred different things, it becomes about nothing. We clarify our theme by noticing how each moment in our story is connected and builds in meaning as it progresses.

Ideas tend to happen at the level of character and plot, such as, "What if my character did this, or that?" Our task is to always be searching for how these actions support our theme.

When we are not entirely clear on our theme, there can also be a tendency to give each idea equal weight. However, if every idea is important, then none of them are. If we want our work to be dynamic, we need to be willing to distill our brilliant ideas down to what is essential. An entire chapter about our protagonist's difficulty parallel parking might be the best writing we have ever done, but unless we explore why his parking struggle is in some way related to the theme, there will be no context for why it belongs in the story.

Our reader is always subconsciously asking, "Why am I being told this? What is the underlying meaning?" Underneath the particular events of our story lies a reason for the telling.

EVERY CHARACTER SERVES A FUNCTION

If a character suddenly vanishes after three chapters, the reader will wonder where he went. If we are not bringing him back, we need to ask ourselves what his function is. Just because we cannot immediately identify a character's function, does not mean there is not one. Before we remove a character, or conflate two characters into one, let's explore what is being expressed through them.

Sometimes, when the tension becomes too great with our antagonists, we conveniently remove them. We may even invent a new character that carries similar traits but allows our protagonist to relate in a less-charged way. For example, if we are writing a story about a battered wife and she gets rid of the husband, only to meet a new guy who eventually treats her in a similar fashion, we must ask ourselves if having two similar antagonists serves our theme or if, indeed, we are avoiding the greater conflict that might ensue if we explored the continuing relationship of the husband. For example, he could return, and the dynamic of how she cannot get rid of him despite her attempts could be explored. Or we might wish to explore the psychology of a woman who does not see the possibility of a better life, and actually allows him to return.

Our story turns on the tension between protagonist and antagonist. If our major antagonist has fallen away by the middle of Act Two, there had better be a good reason. More often than not we temporarily strayed from the central dilemma (it happens to the best of us) and got sidetracked by drama that might not be germane to the theme.

By exploring what might happen if an antagonist is a persistent presence through the entire story, we often see how our story can turn in unexpected ways.

> **TODAY**
> Notice how all of your characters want the same thing and how this leads them into conflict. Notice also where you may have removed a character or a scene as a way to avoid complication. What would happen if you brought the character or the scene back?

Until tomorrow,
Al

DAY 46

"There is no greater agony than bearing an untold story inside you." —MAYA ANGELOU

WHAT IS MY STORY ABOUT?

Hi Writers,

As we approach the middle of our manuscript, our story has likely evolved, and something may have started to happen. It seems paradoxical, but we tend to lose objectivity as we consider the theme of our book. The more deeply we explore that original impulse, the less capable we are of reducing it to a simple idea. That kernel has taken on a life of its own, and now it seems to be about *everything*. It is about forgiveness but it is also about regret, and longing, and betrayal, love, revenge, acceptance, compassion, and on and on. I am not sure why this happens, but I suspect that if we have done our job and our story is alive, then it is going to reflect life in all of its colors. It may seem as if it can no longer contain our *idea* of the story. This is as it should be. Our idea of the story was always limited. The truth of our story is far bigger than what we had initially imagined.

But it is still about something.

Sometimes our story needs to expand before it can become specific. It may feel like we have lost control, but writing a novel is not an intellectual endeavor. Making art is a rebellious undertaking. Something deep within us is taking a stand. We are uniquely qualified to be a channel for this perspective. It can be an exhilarating experience, and at times a lonely one. Somewhere in our subconscious, connections are being made between seemingly disparate ideas in order to reveal a deeper truth. Though our story is a reflection of life in its messy entirety, as we sit patiently with our work and continue to inquire, we recognize patterns that bring us back to our theme.

TODAY
Write for five minutes, beginning with, "My story is about…"
Surprise yourself, and be willing to write the forbidden.

Until tomorrow,
Al

DAY 47

"I like the construction of sentences and the juxtaposition of words – not just how they sound or what they mean, but even what they look like."

—DON DELILLO

JUXTAPOSITION

Hi Writers,

The rewrite process can sometimes lead us into a rut. Our attempts to make our work as clear and specific as possible can begin to feel routine. Sometimes we need to mix things up and get a little dangerous on the page.

David Bowie used to write songs by cutting out words and sticking them together in surprising ways. By randomly arranging words he arrived at juxtapositions that he might never have otherwise considered. Consider his song, "Five years," with the line, "My brain hurt like a warehouse," or a few lines later, "Think I saw you in an ice cream parlor, drinking milkshakes cold and long." These lines may not make much logical sense, yet they are evocative.

There is value in exploring juxtapositions at the level of words, sentences and even plot. Our assumptions about the best way to unravel our story can often limit us from having revelatory experiences. We must not be afraid to mix things up, to take risks and surprise ourselves. In fact, sometimes what is left unsaid provides our story with its meaning. It is often not the words themselves, but the juxtaposition of sentences that ignite the imagination.

Hemingway famously wrote a six-word short story:

"For Sale. Baby shoes. Never worn."

A beginning, middle, and end. Each sentence, on its own has little meaning, but together, it tells a story that is devastating as our imagination fills in the gaps.

TODAY
If your prose is feeling utilitarian, remove every second line from a paragraph and notice how the paragraph reads. Try moving the sentences around randomly. Read them out of order and notice how it alters the meaning.

Until tomorrow,
Al

DAY 48

"I do have trouble with titles."
—JIM HARRISON

WHAT IS THE TITLE OF MY BOOK?

Hi Writers,

This thing we have been typing away at for what seems like forever – what will we call it? Our title can sometimes be the most labor-intensive words of our manuscript. We may have a working title, a placeholder we are using until the heavens part and the right combination of words appears that crystallizes the essence of our story.

Some thoughts:

Consider the tone. The title of a thriller will differ in tone from the title of a comedy. How can we convey the essential feeling of our novel in a word or two? *Bleak House* and *Get Shorty* are tackling different subjects in different ways, which is immediately clear from their respective titles.

Is there a way to suggest the theme without making it explicit? The protagonist's goal or desire could *be* the title, as in Andre Dubus III's *House of Sand and Fog,* or Jonathan Franzen's *Freedom,* or our book could simply be titled after one of our characters, like Nabokov's *Lolita,* Dickens' *David Copperfield* and *Oliver Twist,* and almost everything written by Shakespeare.

We can even tell the reader what the story is about in our title, as in Mark Haddon's *The Curious Incident of the Dog in the Nighttime,* or Suzanne Collins' *The Hunger Games.*

Sometimes a title is only great in retrospect. Sure, it is alliterative, but there is nothing particularly poetic or provocative about *The Great Gatsby,* although it sure beats the titles he considered: *Trimalchio, The High-Bouncing Lover,* and *Under the Red, White and Blue.*

A title can speak directly to our theme, like Ian McEwan's *Atonement* or Dostoevsky's *Crime and Punishment.* It can be blunt and in your face, like Martin Amis' *Money,* as if the book were the final word on the subject, or an irresistible promise, like the A.M. Homes novel, *This Book Will Save Your Life.*

There appears to be no limit to putting the word *America* in titles, such as *American Psycho, American Pastoral,* and *American Gods.* The American Revolution has had many books written about it: *The Glorious Cause, Almost A Miracle,* and many others, yet strangely, they rarely have the word America in the title.

The goal is to get the reader's attention. Book titles are the literary equivalent of headshots for actors. There are no rules for book titles. Tell the story as best you can, and if it is great, even a mundane title like *The Great Gatsby* cannot hurt it.

TODAY
Even if it is just a placeholder, write down a title for your book, and create a title page.

Until tomorrow,
Al

DAY 49

"To sit patiently with a yearning that has not yet been fulfilled, and to trust that that fulfillment will come, is quite possibly one of the most powerful 'magic skills' that human beings are capable of. It has been noted by almost every ancient wisdom tradition."

—ELIZABETH GILBERT

CONTRAST

Hi Writers,

Every story begins with a protagonist's false belief. In *It's a Wonderful Life*, Jimmy Stewart believes that he must leave Bedford Falls in order to have a wonderful life. King Lear believes that the truth lies in flattery. Gatsby believes that he must have Daisy in order to be complete.

Since we are uniquely qualified to write our story, to some degree our protagonist's belief is going to live within us as well. The challenge for us lies in shedding this old belief for a larger truth. It is not that the belief is wrong – it is just that it was never the whole story. Through the story, our protagonist is going to reframe his relationship to this belief.

For example, when Mr. Potter offers Jimmy Stewart a job in the movie *It's a Wonderful Life*, Jimmy declines the offer. But it is important to note that Jimmy initially considers the offer, because if the viewer is to understand the depth of his desire to leave Bedford

Falls, it must be contrasted by his willingness to make a deal with his nemesis. When he chooses to stay, we understand the depth of his loyalty to his town and its citizens.

If Philip Van Doren, author of the short story *The Most Wonderful Gift* (which later became the film, *It's a Wonderful Life*) were to simply have followed his impulses, he might have disregarded the notion that Jimmy would consider Potter's offer, or even that Potter would present him with an offer at all. Why would two enemies want to work together? By exploring our protagonist's temptation, we are led to understand his struggle. Notice how character is revealed through action. Be curious about how you can make your characters more dynamic by showing them in conflict.

We understand character through contrast. Isolation is understood in relation to a desire for connection, loyalty in relation to betrayal, faith in relation to doubt, and courage in relation to fear. Humor is an excellent device in providing contrast. It is essential to infuse our story with humor, particularly if we are writing tragedy. Humor pulls us towards the characters and makes us care. It also ensures that our ending resonates.

Tragedy is not about a death, but about a character recognizing the error of his ways when it is too late. Death is not tragic; it is inevitable. It is the context of the death that illustrates the theme. We can only understand hubris, scheming and vanity if these traits are contrasted in other characters displaying modesty, guilelessness and humility.

TODAY

At the midpoint of your story, notice where your protagonist is tempted. See if you can find a way to make clear his struggle by contrasting his want with what he actually needs. This will make clear his dilemma at this point in the story.

Until tomorrow,
Al

WEEK EIGHT

ACT TWO: PART TWO

At this point in our story the stakes are rising. The story may be turning in a new direction and the challenge in the rewrite is to allow this to happen. We may not have seen the most dynamic possibilities in our first draft, and now, as we glimpse new possibilities for the characters, we may fear that tackling them will collapse our story. This is likely not the case – however, if we are not willing to allow our *idea* of the story to collapse, we may not fully investigate these new possibilities.

QUESTIONS FOR THE WEEK

1. Am I noticing how my protagonist's want never changes while her approach to getting what she wants is constantly changing as the result of her worthy antagonists?

2. Are the stakes rising through complication between my protagonist and her antagonists?

3. How has my protagonist's moment of temptation led her to a deeper commitment?

4. What is specifically at risk as a result of this deeper commitment?

5. Have any possible ties been cut off from my protagonist's past?

DAY 50

"Danger lies in the writer becoming the victim of his own exaggeration, losing the exact notion of sincerity, and in the end coming to despise truth itself as something too cold, too blunt for his purpose – as, in fact, not good enough for his insistent emotion. From laughter and tears the descent is easy to sniveling and giggles." —JOSEPH CONRAD

A WIDER PERSPECTIVE

Hi Writers,

We all have our own story, the one about how we missed the boat, pulled the short straw, the one where we were wronged. Some of us have perfected it over the years, made it bulletproof, unassailable. It is a pretty good story. Heck, sometimes it is even true! However, as storytellers we must remember that every story has an ending.

An ending is simply the natural resolution of a theme. In our personal lives we may go round and round with our own story as it continues to unfold, but in fiction, revisiting the same beat gets old real quick. We are interested in what our protagonist comes to understand as the result of his journey.

As John Gardener states in *On Moral Fiction,* "Everything that happens in fiction leads to a deeper and deeper understanding."

Our story accumulates meaning as it progresses.

In the rewrite we begin to see *why* we wrote what we wrote. At times there can be a tendency to want to soften the drama. Sometimes, as we gain clarity on our protagonist transformed, we begin to squirm at his weaknesses and less attractive qualities, and this can feel embarrassing. We may feel exposed. It is difficult to separate ourselves from our work, even when it is not directly inspired by our own lives (and more so when it is). We might feel a flicker of disgust when we recognize ourselves in our hero and pull back from the conflict when it feels too revealing.

This is a disservice to our story, and it may sound the death knell to all of the great work we did in our first draft. We do not want to neuter the aliveness of our protagonist for some idea of a better man. We love our hero, not because he is good but because he yearns for something more, and unless we show his weaknesses, there will be no context for his shift in perception at the end.

I have noticed in my own rewrite process that when the work begins to get really specific, I start to squirm as I glimpse my limitations. This is where I can withdraw, or I can be curious about my limitations and notice where they live in my characters.

It is sometimes helpful to develop a relationship to our embarrassment. It is natural, the moment we feel ashamed, to shut down. As writers, we cannot afford to do this. If we develop an objective detachment to our work, we will be better equipped to explore our characters.

We are attempting to expose the world, sacred and profane. We may have an idea of what this entails, but our story asks everything of us for a reason. If it did not, we would never surrender. As we shed our old idea of our story, a wider perspective emerges that resolves our protagonist's old belief.

TODAY
Write a scene for five minutes where your protagonist performs his or her darkest secret. Have fun with this, and be willing to write the forbidden.

Until tomorrow,
Al

DAY 51

*"Only those things are beautiful which are inspired by
madness and written by reason."*

—ANDRE GIDE

INSPIRATION

Hi Writers,

There is a madness to this process of allowing our subconscious
to make connections we may not immediately understand. As we
comb through the quick and dirty work of our first draft, we are
emerging from a dream state, and stepping back in order to gain a
more nuanced understanding of all those thousands of words.

Problems may present themselves. We must be careful that we
do not create new problems in our zeal. Solutions are rarely linear,
and yet, when we arrive at one, it is often quite simple, even obvious, in retrospect.

Have you ever tried to remember someone's name, wracking
your brain for days, and then, suddenly while taking a shower, the
name pops into your head? Or, while driving, it hits you why your
last relationship capsized? Suddenly everything makes sense, and
you are left wondering where the insight came from.

Driving, swimming, hiking, rollerblading, doing a puzzle –
these are all right-brain activities, solitary endeavors that do not require great mental effort. When we relax our focus on the *problem,*
new insights tend to emerge.

Rewriting does not all happen at our computer. We are channels for our story. Though we cannot force inspiration, we can create situations where it likes to hang out. Sometimes in the process of putting our work aside and taking a stroll, inspiration arrives.

Right-brain activities are invaluable to the process. Many story problems can be solved on our daily walk.

TODAY
If you are struggling with a story problem, go outside and get some fresh air. The answer comes when you are least expecting it.

Until tomorrow,
Al

DAY 52

"It is error only, and not truth, that shrinks from inquiry."   —THOMAS PAINE

GOING DEEPER

Hi Writers,

Our characters' actions are in service to the essential truth at the heart of our story. We dream in archetypes; the characters in our dreams are always playing out some primal dance. Our subconscious pays no mind to protecting our ego, hence our nightmares.

Our unconscious wants something more than mere survival; it wants us to evolve in spite of our ego. By denying our intuitions we can get out of balance. When this happens our unconscious does not shut down, but rather finds other ways to express itself, whether through distraction, mischief, and even illness. Our unconscious is like a shark – it cannot stop moving. It is constantly searching for resolution. The resolution, at least in story, often lies in the surrendering of some deeply held belief.

In Shakespeare's tragedy, *Romeo and Juliet,* the belief is that we can overcome our family's history. Until this belief is surrendered it is impossible for our heroes to enjoy love. The tragedy lies in their innocent inability to free themselves from this idea.

In many stories, what often separates the hero from the antagonist is that the hero is willing to surrender to the reality of his situation while the antagonist refuses to accept the lesson. We tend to surrender because we have run out of choices, and we recognize that our unwillingness to accept reality can only lead to more suffering. In the moment that we accept the reality of our situation, our suffering tends to subside.

To some degree, we are always writing our own story. It can be helpful to notice where our protagonist's false belief might mirror our own. Our story asks everything of us for a reason. If it did not, we would never surrender the false belief that got us started. It is not that our belief is wrong – it just is not the whole truth.

When we refuse to test our protagonist's core belief through worthy antagonists, our story may feel somewhat vague and will lack the conflict necessary to lead him to a transformation. As storytellers, we cannot afford generalities; good and bad, right and wrong – these terms are vague and lack rigorous inquiry. Story is about cause and effect, action and consequence.

TODAY
What is your protagonist's false belief in the beginning of the story, and how might it be reframed in your ending? Notice how you share that belief. What deeper truth might be revealed if you loosened the reins on this belief?

Until tomorrow,
Al

DAY 53

"We cannot change anything until we accept it. Condemnation does not liberate, it oppresses."

—CARL JUNG

JUDGMENT VERSUS CONDEMNATION

Hi Writers,

Good judgment is an asset. In fact, it is essential in the rewrite process. Problems arise only when we make meaning out of our comparison. When we decide that because we find our work inferior to another writer's work, we ought to quit, we are no longer engaged in our story. We are preoccupied by the result.

It is impossible to remain curious when we are in this space, condemning our work, and sometimes ourselves, rather than taking the objective step back necessary to actually judge it. Judgment is discernment. Condemnation is the negation of possibility, the assumption that the past equals the future. For example, I was a terrible French student. Does that mean I can never learn French? Au contraire.

Good judgment requires a wide perspective. How one disseminates the facts of a situation determines the outcome. Let's say that I do not like a particular passage that I have written. My good judgment may tell me that the passage is general, redundant, and lacking in narrative drive, or a hundred other things. What I do with this information dictates the direction my work takes over the long haul. I can address the problem and search for a solution, or lapse into comparison and list reasons why I never should have begun this blessed chore in the first place.

Guess which one is more productive.

Condemnation leads to despair. We tighten up and the channel closes. Self-consciousness is the fastest way to kill the aliveness of our story. The challenge is to remain curious and be willing to put in the work, even when we are tempted to lapse into self-loathing.

Condemnation is really about fear of change. When it arises, we can ask ourselves where we are being invited to widen our perspective in our story. Is it possible to see our story in a slightly different way? What are our characters trying to tell us?

Sometimes there is no greater fear than true freedom. What if we let go of the idea that we had to figure this thing out on our own? What if we allowed ourselves to follow our characters a little more deeply into the conflict?

Let's say I have written a scene that is not working. By noticing that I am telling myself it is a terrible scene and that my book is a disaster, I might, in fact, be able to have some distance from it. It is not the fear but the meaning I make out of the fear that prevents me from understanding my work in a more specific way. If I can relax enough to break down my condemnation, I might discover that my character shares a similar trait.

TODAY
How can you employ your critical faculties to your advantage by noticing where your judgments live in your characters?

Until tomorrow,
Al

DAY 54

"Change alone is eternal, perpetual, immortal."
—ARTHUR SCHOPENHAUER

CHARACTERS ARE MALLEABLE

Hi Writers,

Our characters are a function of our story. It is important to understand that they are often far more malleable than we may think. The problem arises only when we make our idea of our characters more important than the story. This is where the writer can get lost. Our original impulse is our guiding light. It contains the dilemma, the tension that fuels our story to its conclusion. It is from this place that we rewrite scenes, clarify information, and get down to the dirty work of writing the best novel we can.

All of our revisions are in service to the story as a whole and this must take precedence over material that clouds this goal. When one goes to a good doctor complaining of knee pain, the doctor will examine the hips. He is looking for the *source* of the problem, as opposed to the *apparent* problem.

When we are distracted by the apparent problem, we fail to see the source. For example, let's say that we are writing a story about some yuppie that gets lost on a hike. He is cold and thirsty, night is falling, and he fears that he will not make it to morning. As the author, we may know that he is going to survive, but we want our reader to be unsure. So, let's say that we come to a point in the story where we have run out of ideas and our protagonist is just sitting around, waiting for daybreak. We are stuck. We do not know how to introduce a complication that will heighten the tension. This is where we must be open to altering, or widening, our idea of our character and the story.

Perhaps we originally chose to make him a hiking virgin bereft of wilderness skills. We must remember that as the author we can always introduce elements in the rewrite that help to make our story more dynamic. Perhaps we decide that he is going to build an animal trap to get food, yet we wonder how he might have learned this skill as a tax attorney. Is it possible that he is not a lawyer, but rather an architect with a special skill for building things? Does altering his occupation change the story in any important way? If not, we have now created a character that is more three-dimensional, and not just a construction to support our idea of a yuppie. There is a synchronicity of character and plot. If we set up his technical skills – that he suddenly has this special ability to catch squirrels – early rather than springing it on our reader, the reader will be delighted by the cleverness rather than the convenience.

Perhaps in our first draft we had him hiking alone, but in the rewrite we have him meet someone when he is lost. What if this person is a wanted fugitive and instead of rescuing him, makes his life more difficult? Neither one of these examples would necessarily alter the story's structure, but they could lead to a more specific character and could raise the stakes.

When the impulse is to play it safe and make sure that the story *works,* we may miss opportunities to make the story more dynamic. We must trust that our story can contain all of the seemingly contradictory behaviors of our characters.

I was working with an author who was rewriting a story about a teenage girl who was resentful at her parents for not being allowed to join them on a trip. She said, "My protagonist can't be too angry at her father because she really loves him." But this is just an idea of her protagonist. Is it possible that a fourteen-year-old girl who really loves her father might allow herself to experience the full breadth of her fury *as a result* of the security she feels with him?

TODAY
Do not limit the dynamic possibilities of your characters by being too attached to the outcome of any particular scene.

Until tomorrow,
Al

DAY 55

"Life is banal, but there is a transformation, you see, when you put four edges around it. That changes it. A new world is created. Aside from the fact of just taking things out of context, there is a transformation, and that's fascinating."

—**GARRY WINOGRAND**

CONTEXT

Hi Writers,

As storytellers we are not only building a world, but we are also establishing rules for that world as well. There are internal rules to the world of any story, from *Harry Potter* to *Pride and Prejudice*, and whether we are conscious of it or not, we imbue our work with a point of view. To some degree we do this naturally, instinctively, but cultivating an awareness of this as we rewrite can help us clarify what we are trying to say.

Context allows our reader to suspend her disbelief by providing our story with verisimilitude, a truthfulness that is faithful to the whole. The violence in an Elmore Leonard book is very different than the violence in a Pete Dexter book. When Chili Palmer shoots a bad guy, we are laughing. When Paris Trout has sex with his wife, we are horrified. Once rules have been established they ought not be broken, unless breaking them serves a larger dramatic question – in which case, the exception proves the rule.

There is a rigor to storytelling that is absent in journaling, for example. Whether it is traditionally structured or experimental, a story is about something in particular, and it gathers in meaning as it progresses. Just as a picture has a frame around it, so does a story. Journaling is simply writing down one's thoughts and feelings. It may be explorative, even therapeutic, and might even bear insight that informs one's work, but it is different than crafting a story. Unless we are celebrities and our journals are lusty tell-alls, they will require a thematic context to engage our reader.

Only extremes can fully express the nature of an issue. To explore love through a situation lacking in conflict would not only be dull, it would be *unclear*. We cannot understand a couple's love, except through conflict. If we were to write of a couple holding hands, kissing and fawning over each other, this would not necessarily connote love. It is through conflict that we understand the *nature* of a couple's relationship, whether it is as minor as a couple negotiating household chores or as major as a mother explaining to her child that she and daddy are getting a divorce.

In the rewrite we are constantly guiding the reader's eye, saying, "Look at it this way." Each moment, each scene, is in service to the whole. Without attention to context, our story will drift.

In order to clarify the context, we must be aware of where we place our focus. If too much attention is placed in one area, the reader understandably believes it to be important. For example, notice if you have a character of great significance in the opening of your book who mysteriously vanishes by the end of the first act, without explanation. That may be fine – there are no rules, but we might consider helping our reader understand *why* he is no longer in the story. Our characters are ultimately functions of our story's dramatic question. They exist to clarify what we are attempting to express.

What we are expressing is not the ultimate truth, but rather our perception of the things. When I work with writers, I frequently ask, "Is that true?" I'm not asking if it is true to them, or to the world as a whole, but rather, is it true in the context of the world they have created. That is all that matters.

> **TODAY**
> If a moment in your story feels flat, ask yourself if it is true in the context of the world you have created.

Until tomorrow,
Al

DAY 56

"Only bad writers think that their work is really good."   —JAMES HADFIELD

I AM SO SICK OF MY STORY

Hi Writers,

It is inevitable that we grow sick of our story at some point in the rewrite process. Familiarity breeds contempt. All we see are the mistakes. As we refine our work, our limitations become like a blinking lighthouse signaling the precise areas where it is lacking. When we are in this place it is difficult to have objectivity. We wonder, "Is this just a waste of time...and perhaps a huge embarrassment? How do explain to everyone that this is what I have been spending my time on?" The desire to abandon ship seems to be a part of the process.

Stephen King's wife, Tabitha, found the beginnings of his first novel *Carrie*, in the trash. She read it and encouraged him to finish.

When we are experiencing doubt, it is helpful to ask ourselves a few simple story questions:

- Does my protagonist have a powerful want?

- Do I have worthy antagonists standing in the way of him achieving his goal?

- Do I have something I want to say through these characters, even if I cannot fully articulate it?

If there are days when you feel that every word you have written is worthless and you are tempted to throw the whole thing away, then you're probably a writer.

Franz Kafka asked a friend to burn all of his work before he died. If that friend had not understood the paralyzing self-doubt experienced by all writers, the Kafka canon would have been forever lost.

We would not have been able to get through our first draft if we had allowed ourselves to criticize ever blessed idea, but in the rewrite process, we can afford to take a step back and ask ourselves whether that new scene is actually moving the story forward. We can get up, stretch our legs, and take ten minutes to agonize over whether our protagonist's hair is "leonine" or "Samson-like" if we are so inclined.

The rewrite is where we embrace our objectivity. We let go of the idea that this work must be a masterpiece. Our job is to let it live. Ironically, when we approach our work with a certain cool detachment we tend to write from a place of greater truth.

TODAY
Rather than dining out on your self-doubt, notice where it lives in your protagonist and you will begin to see how you are uniquely qualified to write your story.

Until tomorrow,
Al

WEEK NINE

OUR HERO SUFFERS

This week we are rewriting up to the point where our protagonist suffers. Certainly our hero struggles in a variety of ways throughout the story, but what makes the moment of suffering unique is that his suffering is due to an awakening sense of the underlying dilemma. He is beginning to see that what he set out to accomplish may be far more difficult than he had imagined.

There is a difference between struggling and suffering. We struggle when we are faced with a difficult task. We suffer when we sense that our goal may be impossible, but we are not yet ready to surrender the meaning we have attached to it.

In the film *Rocky*, the moment of suffering occurs when the protagonist begins training for the big fight. He runs up the steps for the first time, clutching his side in pain, and realizes that he is in terrible shape. He has committed to fight the champ but now realizes that he may have set himself up for a terrible defeat. The moment of suffering often rises directly out of the choice that our protagonist made at the midpoint. Now that he has walked through temptation and become fully committed, he is beginning to understand the impossibility of achieving his goal. It is not simply that Rocky fears he will lose the fight, but rather he believes that if he does not win it means he is a bum and therefore not worthy of Adrien's love.

Remember, the story points are not simply about what happens, i.e. plot, but the meaning we ascribe to what happens, i.e. theme.

The moment of suffering can be one of the most elusive story points and, as such, is frequently where we get derailed in our first draft. Sometimes the second half of our second act feels underwritten or we feel vague about what we are attempting to express. When we focus on trying to raise the stakes, we tend to manufacture conflict that is not intrinsic to the story. But by exploring our protagonist's driving want, and noticing how it is in direct conflict to what he needs, an image may emerge that serves to raise the stakes.

The moment of suffering is the penultimate story point of Act Two, preceding our hero's surrender. The moment of suffering is crucial because it provides context for what is approaching. We do not typically surrender until we have exhausted all of our options. The moment of suffering is often where our protagonist realizes that this is his last chance. Where is the potential for this moment in our story? The purpose of exploring this moment is to find the most dynamic way to explore our protagonist's dilemma.

QUESTIONS FOR THE WEEK:

1. How can I show that there is no going back for my hero, despite his realization that his goal is more difficult than he imagined?

2. What does it look like when my protagonist suffers?

3. How do my antagonists lead to my protagonist's suffering?

4. What is the most dynamic way to explore this moment?

5. Is it possible that my protagonist is beginning to recognize the dilemma of his situation at this point? How can I show this?

DAY 57

"Art must take reality by surprise."
—FRANCOISE SAGAN

THE ART OF REVELATION

Hi Writers,

Every comedian understands the element of surprise. They save the punch line for the end. Every piece of information, every misdirection, is in service to the punch line having its greatest effect. Where and when we reveal information can have a profound effect on our narrative.

When I wrote the first draft of *Diamond Dogs*, I revealed that Neil's father was the sheriff early on. This meant that when Neil arrived home with the body in the trunk, we already knew that his father was a lawman. This sort of spoiled the fun. I thought, what if I revealed this as his father greeted him in the garage when he arrives home? It has greater impact if we discover this at the moment we understand all that it means. It is a way of focusing our reader's attention, and it is also just really fun storytelling. Don't we want our reader to be biting his nails, and wondering where the hell we are taking them on this journey?

Explore the precise moment of revelation for the greatest effect.

Surprises can happen on many different levels. We can explore misdirections within scenes, where the scene appears to be moving in one direction, and then goes in another direction. For example, if we know the scene is going to end with our hero proposing to his girlfriend, it could begin with his intention to break up. This is not manipulation or milking the scene, it is a way of conveying our protagonist's dilemma in the most specific way. This is what happens in life.

Tension and release.

Providing our reader with surprises is not only a way to keep him reading, but it is also a means of keeping him connected.

TODAY
Where you choose to reveal information can alter the pace and meaning of your story. Are your story's revelations placed as effectively as possible?

Until tomorrow,
Al

DAY 58

"The story I am writing exists, written in absolutely perfect fashion, some place, in the air. All I must do is find it, and copy it."   —JULES RENARD

NOTICING PATTERNS

Hi Writers,

We are always asking ourselves what our story is *about*. Let's not wrack our brains for the "right answer" but rather approach it from a place of wonder. It is a question for the heart and not the head.

We may notice how all of the characters in our story revolve around a particular dilemma; they all have a relationship to this dilemma, whether it is their ambition at war with their integrity, their desire for love at war with their need for autonomy, their desire for validation at war with their need for authenticity, and on and on. The patterns inform the dilemma that our characters struggle with.

Our characters are functions of our story and the patterns that we notice offer clues to help us understand our story in a more specific way. This is what makes the rewrite so exciting; we are engaged in a process of making our story bigger than we are by becoming conscious of the underlying patterns.

So, what is our story about? Is it about freedom, revenge, finding true love? What is the nature of these conditions? As we hold up our ideas of the way things are against what our subconscious seeks to resolve, we begin to shed some of our old ideas of the way our story ought to go.

The rewrite is a mysterious process of distilling a seemingly infinite number of elements down to something that amounts to a greater truth. Everything that happens in our story, all of the patterns are leading to our ending, the resolution of the dilemma.

TODAY
Your ending informs everything that precedes it. If a moment or scene is feeling general or aimless, look at your ending and track the story backwards from that place.

Until tomorrow,
Al

DAY 59

"In the best fiction, plot is not a series of surprises but an increasingly moving series of recognitions, or moments of understanding."   —JOHN GARDNER

LETTING GO OF THE PLOT

Hi Writers,

Writing a story is a setup. We begin, excited by what the story promises, only to realize that completion requires a tad more insight and courage than we may currently possess. It is easy to become bogged down by fear as we face the mountain of work still ahead. We are straddling two worlds: our current existence, and a place of new possibility just beyond our imagination.

We tend to get caught up in thinking that our story is all about the plot. It feels that way when we are faced with the consuming question of "What happens next?" We may find ourselves distracted, trying to *perfect* our prose in an effort to avoid the real problem. We may hope that if the *writing* is good enough nobody will notice that we are *forcing* the story. However, when we approach our story from a surrendered place, the plot has a way of revealing itself in ways we might never have imagined.

Writing is an act of faith. We trust that there is some kind of order to the universe, that there is a satisfactory resolution to the dilemma at the heart of our story.

If we are getting stuck halfway through our work, it may be because we are clinging to our *idea* of the plot. This can be painful. I have known people who have held onto their idea for decades.

To move forward in our work, we need to recognize our rightful place in the process. Yes, daydreaming about publication, advances, agents, and how amazing that book tour will be is frankly, inevitable. But it is not productive.

TODAY
Let go of the idea that you are supposed to figure out how your story should go.

Until tomorrow,
Al

DAY 60

"In art the hand can never execute anything higher than the heart can inspire."
—RALPH WALDO EMERSON

WHERE DOES THIS LIVE IN MY STORY?

Hi Writers,

When I began outlining my novel *Diamond Dogs,* I did not know that the father was going to dispose of the body – an action that became the cornerstone of the book! For a long time I assumed that Neil, the son, would dispose of the body and never speak of it to his father, the town sheriff. But the more I wondered about their relationship and sensed that they shared a secret from the past, the more I moved toward the possibility of allowing this new idea to take root. I knew it was a story about family secrets. One day this plot revelation simply presented itself and the story began falling into place.

As we delve into our characters, we experience their impulses, which in turn inform their actions. We must trust these impulses, even if they seem at odds with our original conception of the story. We might expect that a sheriff who discovers a dead body would seek justice, or at the very least question his implicated son about it. And yet that expectation did not ring true emotionally in my story, which is the most important logic to keep in mind as we write.

As I made this major change in the plot, I understood more clearly what I was actually trying to say. I realized that this was a story about how cycles are broken. It felt like I had known it all along, but was just resisting, that perhaps I had dismissed the change because I was not ready for it yet.

Though we may be quite sure of the direction our story should go, when we hold our idea of the story loosely, our perspective widens. Our impulses often differ from our idea of how the story should go. When we trust our impulses and ask, "Where does this live in the world of my story?" we are often led to a fresh perspective.

TODAY
Watch for where your story feels incomplete and notice the characters' impulses in these places. Are you simply trying to advance the plot or are you trusting your characters and being true to their dilemma?

Until tomorrow,
Al

DAY 61

"Deep unspeakable suffering may well be called a baptism, a regeneration, the initiation into a new state."   —GEORGE ELIOT

SUFFERING AND SURRENDER

Hi Writers,

Sometimes writers confuse the hero's suffering with the moment of surrender, but these are actually two distinct stages of his journey.

We surrender because we are confronted with the impossibility of ever getting what we want. There is a world of difference between struggling to get what we want, and the moment we realize the impossibility of achieving it. When we struggle, we dig in our heels, we tighten up, our focus narrows. However, a certain relief comes with surrender. Though there may be grief, it is the end of a struggle and offers the opportunity to move on.

Until the hero surrenders, he will not reframe his relationship to what he wants. Reframing his relationship to his desire is where the magic is. It is sort of like the difference between fundamentalism and creativity. Fundamentalists do not believe anything needs to be reframed. They believe the answer has already been revealed, therefore we must simply hold on and wait, and those who hold an opposing view risk banishment. That is the power of fundamentalism; it threatens our primal desire to belong and promises reward at a later time, as if freedom were unattainable now.

It takes courage to be a writer. We are committing ourselves to a search that is not supported by polite society. The storyteller seeks freedom. This is what makes writers so threatening. In the 1950s, at the height of the Cold War hysteria, when Senator McCarthy wanted to make the world safe from Communists, he primarily went after writers. In frightening times, the majority's impulse is to silence the voice of dissent even if that voice cries out for equality, compassion, forgiveness, and true freedom. The concept of freedom is sacrilege to those who bow to an unquestioned authority. The ignorant prefer misery rather than risk exile.

Surrender is not passive. The dark night of the soul is a rite of passage that eventually leads to dawn. It allows us to glimpse the possibility of true freedom.

TODAY
A lot happens between the moment your protagonist suffers and her moment of surrender. If the story feels thin here, notice the difference in these two experiences. One demands that you cling dearly to an old belief, while the other is willing to let everything go. What particular events must happen in order to arrive at surrender?

Until tomorrow,
Al

DAY 62

"A beautiful thing is never perfect."
—PROVERB

THE PERFECT BOOK

Hi Writers,

Fear, doubt, and impatience: all sorts of demons spring up as we rewrite. We may attempt to ward them off in a number of ways: attempting to dazzle our reader with showy prose, trying to *make sense* of our characters and ultimately denying them any chance for a flesh and blood presence by ignoring their initial impulses, or daydreaming about the result instead of doing our work.

There is a term that some critics like to use because it makes them sound smart. They like to dub a piece of work *near perfect*, with the tacit implication that they alone possess the insight into how it could have been flawless. This kind of language can subtly insinuate itself into the psyche of the artist, setting up a vague and impossible goal. As artists, when we seek perfection we become paralyzed and can sometimes kill what is so imperfectly alive. Speaking of art in terms of perfection misses the point.

When we strive for perfection we tend to focus on the result. We can become paralyzed by fear, losing connection to our voice.

Strive for excellence, not perfection.

Rather than concerning ourselves with all of the perceived

flaws, let's get excited about the moments of aliveness in our story and have the courage to work from beginning to end.

> **TODAY**
> Is your goal to make the work alive and specific, or are you attempting to make your work universally beloved and unassailable to critics? The former is a worthy goal. The latter is a setup for failure. Write down your greatest fear in completing your book. Now notice where this identical fear lives in your protagonist. Rather than trying to figure out how to make your work good, explore how this fear contributes to your hero's suffering.

Until tomorrow,
Al

DAY 63

*"The problems of the world cannot possibly be solved
by skeptics or cynics whose horizons are limited by
the obvious realities. We need men who can dream
of things that never were."*   —JOHN F. KENNEDY

THE *PROBLEM* IS ALWAYS CHANGING

Hi Writers,

Throughout our story our protagonist's apparent problem is always
changing. For example, in *Diamond Dogs*, Neil kills a boy on the
highway. He has a problem: *"Do I tell someone, or do I cover it up?"*
He decides to hide the body. When his father discovers the body, a
new problem presents itself. *"What does it mean that my father is
remaining silent?"* When his father disposes of the body for him,
Neil is presented with yet another problem, this time less immediate and even more troubling, *"I am bonded to my father by this
secret."* An FBI agent shows up and starts asking questions. The plot
is propelled forward and the dilemma becomes more complicated
as new problems arise, one after the other.

The dilemma is that as long as one keeps secrets, one can never have a true connection to others. As Neil struggles with trying
to keep himself safe, he becomes increasingly isolated from his
schoolmates until his dearest friend, in an attempt to protect Neil,
is arrested for the crime.

The problem continues to change right up until the climax of the story where the dilemma is resolved. The dilemma is resolved when the protagonist makes a new choice. The new choice is that Neil confronts his father about his past and in doing so the truth emerges. But this is not the actual battle scene. The battle scene for Neil happens when he suddenly sees his father in a new way. He understands the reason for his father's rage and he is able to forgive him. The forgiveness comes from a place of true understanding.

TODAY
Notice how every scene in your story is leading inexorably to the climax where the dilemma is ultimately resolved.

Until tomorrow,
Al

WEEK TEN

THE HERO SURRENDERS

This week we are rewriting up to the end of Act Two where our protagonist surrenders the possibility of achieving his goal. Through this surrender he experiences a death of his old identity and reframes his relationship to his goal.

In the rewrite it is helpful to not only recognize where this moment lives in our story but also to inquire into the meaning that our protagonist makes out of his goal. It is not the protagonist's goal that gets surrendered but the meaning he attaches to it. By exploring not only how but why it is impossible to achieve his goal, we are often led to a more specific relationship to the end of Act Two.

Why is it impossible for our protagonist to achieve his goal? The answer does not lie in a physical situation, although it may appear so. The impossibility springs from a deeper place. It is something primal.

There is no need to manufacture this moment, but only to make it as clear and specific as possible. The end of Act Two is the linchpin of the story. The story turns on this point, and without clarity on the dilemma it can careen off the rails.

QUESTIONS FOR THE WEEK:

1. What event happens that leads my protagonist to recognize the impossibility of achieving his goal?

2. At this point in the story what has my protagonist lost, and what must he let go of?

3. What is the meaning that he made out of his goal?

4. How does he reframe his goal?

5. How does reframing his goal alter his outlook?

DAY 64

"There is no dilemma compared with that of the deep-sea diver who hears the message from the ship above, 'Come up at once. We are sinking.'"

—ROBERT COOPER

PROBLEM VERSUS DILEMMA

Hi Writers,

In surrendering to the impossibility of achieving her goal, our protagonist is able to approach her *apparent problem* from a new perspective, and in doing so, the dilemma often resolves itself. Although our protagonist's dilemma never changes, the problem is constantly changing. As she solves one problem a new one takes its place. This is why a dilemma cannot exist without a worthy antagonist. Unless we have powerful antagonists standing in the way of our protagonist achieving her goal, she will never experience a dark night of the soul, which will force her to challenge the meaning she attached to her goal. It is only in reframing her relationship to the goal that she will be led to the resolution of her dilemma.

Another way to think of it is this: problem is plot, while dilemma is subtext. Plot addresses the immediate problem, while the dilemma is the thing boiling underneath it. Our protagonist often does not realize that she is facing a dilemma because she is so intent on solving the problem directly in front of her. Awakening to the dilemma she is facing is a key part of the hero's journey.

Because story is the exploration of a theme, and our characters are all functions of that theme, we may notice that all of our characters want the same thing. This may sound crazy. We might say, "No they don't. Ted wants to be in a relationship with Susan, and Susan does not want to have anything to do with him." But if we dig deeper, we begin to locate their shared desire. Perhaps it is that they both want love or to be validated or to be adored. It is precisely because they perceive their situation differently that their shared desire leads to the ensuing drama.

The conflict arises precisely because they want the same thing, yet they perceive their goal in different ways.

Here are some examples of shared goals between protagonists and antagonists:

1. In Jonathan Franzen's *Freedom*, the husband and wife both seek love from people who are incapable or reciprocating. For the husband, it is his wife, and for the wife, it is the character of Richard.

2. In Patti Smith's memoir, *Just Kids*, she and Robert Mapplethorpe both seek to express themselves through their art but for different reasons. Patti seeks connection while Robert seeks escape.

3. In *King Lear*, the protagonist seeks a worthy heir while his three daughters wish to be seen as such. The drama results from the different ways these characters attempt to achieve this goal.

TODAY
Stay connected to your protagonist's dilemma, while remaining curious to the myriad ways she attempts to solve the problems in front of her.

Until tomorrow,
Al

DAY 65

"The art of love is largely the art of persistence."
—ALBERT ELLIS

WE HAVE AUTHORITY OVER OUR WORK

Hi Writers,

There can be a desire to want to erase something because we do not quite understand it, or we fear that we are not up to the task of making it clear. When we are faced with this, the more challenging choice is to be patient and trust that our subconscious will resolve it in time.

Sometimes what we write is so personal that we fear nobody will understand. When we feel exposed, we are hitting pay dirt. Tapping into the universal is terrifying, but also liberating. It is uncomfortable because it is unfamiliar, but as we stay with it, clarity will prevail.

> **TODAY**
> Ask yourself the following questions, and note that a section may mean a sentence, paragraph or an entire chapter:
> 1. Is this section necessary?
> 2. What would I lose by removing it?
> 3. What is essential in this section?
> 4. Can I remove the section and layer what is essential into other areas of my story?

Until tomorrow,
Al

DAY 66

*"Don't worry about what the world needs. Ask what
makes you come alive, and go do it. Because what
the world needs are people who have come alive."*
—HOWARD THURMAN

THE INNER CRITIC

Hi Writers,

There is a difference between writing for our ideal reader and writing for our inner critic. The inner critic is like a 24-hour flu – it passes, but in the meantime it has prevented us from doing our work. The challenge is to write *through* the fear.

If we rewrite from our inner critic, we can kill the aliveness of our work. If we second-guess ourselves, we can create a decade-long battle from what should have been a three-month polish.

Creating art requires that we accept the work for what it is. We cannot force our characters to be other than they are. Just as water goes with the flow, our characters adhere to the context within which we have placed them.

When we trust our characters' impulses, we often find ourselves pleasantly surprised that their behavior is still in service to our theme. The moment we try to impose a false action on our characters, they will rebel.

So how do we reconcile trusting the aliveness of our characters with adhering to our story's underlying theme? Being aware of the tension between these two seemingly opposing forces is half the battle.

It is a matter of focus. If we focus on the road directly in front of our car when driving on the highway, our control of the vehicle is limited, but if we widen our perspective, the car moves more smoothly, and we are able to relax. Storytelling works the same way. We move from the general to the specific.

It is our job to listen to our characters, which requires patience. Sometimes we will receive inspiration in great hunks, sometimes it comes in dribs and drabs. We take it when we can get it. We try to be grateful and remember that inspiration is the result of sincere inquiry.

The inner critic wants us to fail. It cannot stand the tension of waiting to see if the cake will rise. It may be the worst part of ourselves but that does not mean that we cannot use it to our advantage.

The only way to silence our inner critic is to continue to do our work in spite of it and to make our story more important than the result. The antidote is not to steel ourselves from our insecurity, but to inquire into its nature. We are going to experience ups and downs but if we can ride the waves without making too much meaning out of the experience, we will be led to a more specific version of our story.

TODAY
Notice how your fear speaks to you and you will discover how it speaks to your protagonist.

Until tomorrow,
Al

DAY 67

"I see people in terms of dialogue and I believe that people are their talk."   —RODDY DOYLE

DIALOGUE

Hi Writers,

There is a difference between real life dialogue and fictive dialogue. Fictive dialogue always works to a purpose, revealing character, backstory, conflict, subtext, motive and theme. If it is really good, it does all of these things at once, while appearing to sound like real life.

Writers struggle with dialogue when they believe their characters ought to speak even when they have nothing to say. People only speak when they *want* something.

Sometimes we use dialogue to force exposition. It is unkind to make our characters say things they would never say.

What people say is rarely what they mean, and when they do in fiction, it probably does not need to be said. Look for ways to show rather than tell. When a character says, *I love you,* it might mean: "do you love me?" or "I hate you," or "I want your money." And it might mean all of these things at once.

The key to writing great dialogue is having a strong connection to the subtext. The subtext is the unspoken world of the scene, which is revealed through action. By being connected to our characters' underlying motives, our dialogue begins to crackle with the energy of that which wants to be said but is forbidden. If our dialogue feels flat, or expository, or if our characters all sound the same, we can ask ourselves some questions:

- What is the conflict in the scene? Every scene in our story has conflict, including love scenes...especially love scenes.

- What is the backstory? What has led these characters to this particular moment? The more we know about the world of our story, the richer the moment will be.

- What is at stake? What do the characters want? Remember, all of our characters want something and the stakes are always life and death. If our protagonist does not get what he wants, his life will be unimaginable.

- What are the various ways the characters attempt to get what they want?

- What is the dilemma, and how are all of these characters connected to it?

- How can I relate the information the reader needs to understand without forcing the characters to tell it? We never want a character to say, "Oh look, it's my Grandma Martha who I have not seen in 20 years because I have been in prison for robbing that bank." Allow the information to be revealed through conflict.

- Do all of my characters sound alike? If I remove all the characters' names from the dialogue, will my reader still know who is speaking?

TODAY
What makes your characters' distinctive? We all have different rhythms and cadences, speech patterns and verbal ticks. We are of different classes, religions, ethnicities, and levels of education. Some people have a poetic style, while others are brusque and abrasive. Allow your characters to sound different by focusing on one particular trait in each of them. Surprise yourself with what arises.

Until tomorrow,
Al

DAY 68

"The very essence of instinct is that it's followed independently of reason."   —CHARLES DARWIN

INSTINCT VERSUS IDEA

Hi Writers,

I was working with a writer who was concerned that her hero was too whiny in the first act. In the rewrite there can be a tendency for the writer to try and *solve* an apparent problem by killing the *aliveness* of the work. It is an understandable concern that her protagonist be likeable, but rather than concerning herself with whether or not the character is being whiny, she might explore the reason for her whininess by looking at what her protagonist wants. The whininess could be a function of the character trying to achieve her goal or it could be an indication that the conflict is not strong enough. There is no such thing as too whiny. The writer may not need to make the character less whiny but rather to explore the obstacles that she is up against, her worthy antagonists. If a character complains about the soup to a guard in Auschwitz, is this whining or bravery? Or perhaps the whining is outsized in response to her current circumstance and is a manifestation of an earlier time when only the squeaky wheel got the grease. Be curious about *why* the character is behaving the way she is behaving, and look for antagonistic forces that support this behavior rather than assuming the behavior is wrong.

We must trust our instincts and question our ideas.

The instinct was to write the whining. The idea is that she is too whiny. The instinct recognizes that there is a problem. If we solve our idea of the problem we will destroy all of our good work. But if we continue to trust our instinct, our work goes deeper.

TODAY
Do not be distracted by the appearance of your characters' situations. Explore the reason for their struggles.

Until tomorrow,
Al

DAY 69

"You will, I am sure, agree with me that if page 534 only finds us in the second chapter, the length of the first one must have been really intolerable."
—ARTHUR CONAN DOYLE

WHERE DO MY CHAPTERS END?

Hi Writers,

Many of us wrote our first draft quickly, unconcerned with chapter breaks. In the rewrite, we may wonder how to divide our book into readable sections.

The purpose of a chapter break is like an intermission in a play. We are giving our reader a place to take a break. Some authors write chapters that are roughly equal in length while others write books, like Thomas Harris' *Hannibal*, that vary from a dozen pages to a single paragraph. There are novelists that have written books with no chapter breaks at all and no one has put them in author jail.

Although there are no rules, here are some points to consider.

A chapter may end with a lingering question or cliffhanger, something that compels the reader to find out what happens next.

Chapters tend to end when a scene ends. Just as a sentence explores a single thought and a paragraph explores a topic, a chapter is often like a short story within a larger story, with its own beginning, middle and end.

If a chapter begins in the present, and then lapses into backstory, consider bookending the scene by completing the chapter back in the present. Otherwise the reader may lose the story thread.

Some books have numbered chapter breaks, while other books have chapter titles. If our story is told from multiple narrators, we might consider giving each narrator his or her own chapter as Russell Banks does in his novel, *Continental Drift*.

We may have written an epic novel where simply breaking it up into chapters is not enough. It might require being sectioned off into parts, with each part having its own series of chapters. The parts can be a way of dividing the novel up into act breaks, or major turning points, or each part can indicate a different time period or a new locale.

Ultimately, the decision is an intuitive one. Each story has its own unique way of being read.

TODAY
Taking no more than one hour, go through your manuscript and break it down into chapters. These chapter breaks may change, but this will begin to give you a sense of the pacing of your book.

Until tomorrow,
Al

DAY 70

"Our dilemma is that we hate change and love it at the same time; what we really want is for things to remain the same but get better."
                                    —Sydney Harris

REFRAMING THE GOAL

Hi Writers,

Sometimes writers ask me if they are doing it right which endows me with an authority I do not possess, and implies that there are rules. There are no rules.

At the end of Act Two, the dilemma becomes apparent to our protagonist. He consciously understands that he is being pulled in two different directions, thus making his goal impossible to achieve. He realizes that he cannot win, that in fact, the meaning he has made out of his goal has actually prevented the possibility of achieving it. Consider this: If we want love because we think it will make us whole, we will never find love, because we are already whole. If we want to be successful so that we will feel validated, no amount of success will satisfy our craving, because we were okay all along. Until we give ourselves what we need, we will forever be in bondage to what we want. By reframing our relationship to our goal it becomes possible to achieve it if it belongs in our life. It is not that our protagonist cannot have love or success, it is just that until he realizes that these goals do not define him, he will never recognize what he has.

It is through this new understanding that our protagonist is able to begin to give himself what he needs. In spite of the lack of external love or validation, our protagonist moves toward giving himself what he needs in Act Three.

In accepting the reality of his situation, the protagonist lets go of the possibility of ever getting what he wants. This does not mean that he no longer has these desires. We never stop wanting love, or success, but by reframing our relationship to these desires, they no longer rule us.

TODAY

Notice the moment at which your protagonist recognizes the impossibility of achieving his goal. How has he run out of choices? What does this moment mean to him, and how will he reframe this meaning so that he can begin to give himself what he needs?

Until tomorrow,
Al

WEEK ELEVEN

OUR HERO ACCEPTS
THE REALITY OF HIS SITUATION

This week we are rewriting through approximately one third of our Third Act. Many things are happening to our protagonist simultaneously at this point in the story. As a result of his surrender he has reframed his relationship to the meaning he attached to his goal, and in doing so he is becoming aware of the reality of his situation. The reality is a bedrock understanding of what he is actually dealing with. The smoke has cleared and oftentimes the hero understands that to attack the problem head on is fruitless. He cannot vanquish his antagonists through force of will. He must accept that what he is dealing with is mightier than he is.

By accepting the reality of his situation our protagonist is humbled and, paradoxically, through this experience he glimpses new possibilities. In Act Three he begins to understand what his situation *means*. When we read books or watch movies we are seeking meaning. We may think that we are just following the plot, but the purpose of the plot is simply to maintain verisimilitude. We will buy without question whatever is set up – wizards, vampires, or a magical world down a rabbit hole – however, once the rules of the world have been established they cannot be broken. If our story goes off in a direction that is not germane to the theme, the audience will sense it instantly. The challenge of Act Three is to remain true to the world that we have set up by continually returning to our story's underlying meaning.

Consider why we reread a book or watch a movie for a second time. Since we already know what happens, are we revisiting the story for its plot, or are we seeking to *re-experience* it? Is it possible that on some level the story's meaning changes each time we revisit it? How can a book or a film offer us a different experience when the writer has not changed a word and the filmmaker has not altered a single frame? Is it perhaps because *we have changed?* A six-year-old child's experience of reading *How the Grinch Stole Christmas* is quite different than her parent's experience, which is different than her grandparent's experience, because we bring the sum total of who we are to our experiences. In other words, our perception of a situation is altered based upon who we are. In Act Three our protagonist re-frames his relationship to his goal based upon who he has become as the result of his struggles in Act Two. His perspective has widened and he is now seeing his situation in a new way.

In rewriting Act Three we become the wise man or woman on the hill. In recognizing the impossibility of solving his problem, our protagonist becomes willing to face what he was previously avoiding, and in doing so, his relationship to his goal changes.

QUESTIONS FOR THE WEEK:

1. What possible revelation does my protagonist experience at this point in the story?

2. How does this revelation alter his perception of his situation?

3. What has my protagonist been avoiding that he is now willing to confront as the result of this revelation?

4. What does my protagonist understand about his goal now that he did not understand at the beginning?

5. How does this understanding cause him to take action?

6. How has this understanding altered his relationships to the antagonists?

DAY 71

"And the day came when the risk to remain tight in a bud was more painful than the risk it took to blossom."   —ANAIS NIN

THE TRUE NATURE OF OUR CHARACTERS

Hi Writers,

Good writing is a synthesis of ideas and instincts working in concert. Whenever the writer is bound by either one of these elements, he is out of balance. We have been indoctrinated to believe that *good writing* is a skill rather than a practice. When we are connected to the aliveness of our characters' internal conflict, our writing becomes compelling and unpredictable.

Let's say, for instance, that we envision our hero getting increasingly frustrated with the antagonist throughout the story, but when we explore the nature of *increasingly frustrated,* we see that it actually looks different than we had imagined. In the course of one's frustration, one might excuse oneself from the situation, and then feel guilty for leaving. Or question why he is so impatient. Or struggle between self-doubt and growing fury. In short, frustration contains a multitude of experiences that cannot strictly be called *frustration.* Mounting frustration is a process and may contain an infinite number of emotional colors, all of which vary depending on the characters in question and the overarching dilemma that preoccupies them.

Our character's frustration is particular to his situation. By exploring the specifics of his particular conflict, we are led beyond our *idea* of frustration. In fact, in the rewrite we may discover that this character experiences rage, apology, embarrassment, soul-searching, despair, hopefulness, excitement, grief, suspicion, madness and even gratitude at his current situation. The nature of a frustrating experience may differ greatly from our idea of what it means to feel frustrated.

The protagonist of Joseph Heller's *Catch-22* wants to return home. He is stuck, fearing for his life in a distant war-torn country, and is only permitted to leave if he can prove that he is mentally unstable. But this is war! To say that he is scared is proof of his sanity. To say that he wants to continue flying dangerous missions is praised as patriotic. Either way, he is not going home. As the story progresses, we experience the hero's mounting frustration as a result of his hope, awareness, grief and despair.

We are always seeking balance. In doing so we can overcompensate, and this produces drama. There is often a difference between our preconceived notion of a character's experience and the true nature of that experience. For instance, the nature of passivity includes rage. The nature of confidence includes insecurity. The nature of hatred includes love and vice versa.

By exploring the nature of our characters' experiences, our character's internal struggle becomes more truthful and dynamic. This is crucial to consider in Act Three. Just because our protagonist is aware of his dilemma does not mean he is without conflict. His situation continues to be dire as he struggles to find his way back home.

There can be a tendency in the third act to steer our protagonist away from mounting conflict by endowing him with wisdom he has not earned. This robs our story of rich drama in Act Three. Wisdom is not merely a function of self-knowledge but a willingness to make a new choice in spite of one's old beliefs.

TODAY
1. In Act Three, pick a scene that feels flat or where your protagonist is passive.
2. Identify what she wants in the scene and the obstacles standing in the way of her achieving her goal.
3. Write down the variety of experiences she might endure in her attempt to achieve her goal.
4. Notice where these experiences might belong in the scene.

Until tomorrow,
Al

DAY 72

"Logic is neither an art nor a science but a dodge."
—STENDHAL

BUILDING A COHERENT NARRATIVE

Hi Writers,

In the first draft we write fast, searching for the story and trying to outrun those demons that insist we are unqualified for the task. As we reread, we find some material that we like and some we do not. In any case, there is always something to work with. It can be overwhelming, however, when we confront the various logistical discrepancies and contradictions: my hero might be thirty-years old in the beginning and seventy-five years old at the end, yet only two months have elapsed in the narrative. As we confront these discrepancies, we fear they might bury us.

Au contraire.

Story problems are not meant to be figured out. They are often invitations to get more specific, and will almost inevitably lead to a richer version of our story. As we explore the underlying nature of the discrepancies, we begin to see what our subconscious was trying to express. We have come this far trusting our right brain. Now is not the time to neuter our story by making logical choices. Our characters rarely behave logically. As a matter of fact, one definition of drama might be *characters behaving uncharacteristically*. When we look at our story, is it not full of characters behaving in ways that surprise other characters and themselves?

Sometimes we are so adamant about what must happen in a particular scene that we lose connection to the scene's larger purpose. There are often a variety of ways to say the same thing. We must not limit our options by insisting that our characters behave a certain way.

TODAY
1. Identify a scene that contains a logic problem or "hole."
2. Rather than trying to solve the "problem," explore the possibility of a character making a different or opposite choice in the scene.
3. Notice how this may widen your relationship to the character and thus shift your understanding of the scene.

Until tomorrow,
Al

DAY 73

"I can't go on. I'll go on."
—SAMUEL BECKETT

WE ARE A CHANNEL

Hi Writers,

We have good writing days and bad ones. On good days, it feels like the wind is at our backs and we are being guided. On bad days we are convinced that we should scrap the whole endeavor. There can be a tendency to make a big deal out of these highs and lows, but I am not sure they go away. Over time we are just less inclined to take them seriously.

Our insights can take a while to sink in. A new insight can be met with elation, "Eureka! Now I have the answer!" And the next day can be a letdown as we realize it was not *the answer*, just *an answer*, and we return to our rightful place as channels for the story. But this is good news. It takes the heat off.

Years ago, I was working as a standup comic in San Francisco and spending my days locked in my hotel room writing fiction. I had been stuck at a point in my third act for days and was growing increasingly frustrated as I tried to figure out how to resolve it. I wanted the two characters to realize that they loved each other, but I could not seem to get them to come together. They were both trapped in their fears and unwilling to break out of it. Finally, in a fit of frustration, I put on my jacket and went out for some fresh air. I skulked along Fisherman's Wharf and then up to the Presidio, with my head down, bemoaning my sorely limited skills. And then, I looked up and noticed that I was standing in a park, at the top of a hill, watching the sun set over the Golden Gate Bridge. I suddenly felt this intense wave of emotion. I had become so distracted by the importance of completing my work that I had lost connection to why I was telling the story in the first place.

Suddenly my story didn't matter so much. Clearly it was beyond my abilities and besides, how was I going to figure out love? Instead, I just stood there and watched the sun set. As I began to relax, I realized that the two characters came together because they needed each other. Love wasn't a negotiation. It wasn't something that was measured and quantified. It is a primal force, moving us inexorably towards each other, regardless of our fears. In that moment my ending began to appear to me. It still took some time. There were still more anxieties, but I was on the other side of it as I realized I didn't have to figure it out.

I spent my first decade as a writer approaching the work the way my siblings had approached medical school. I slaved doggedly, incessantly, struggling to perfect my craft. But writing is different than studying for midterms. We are channels for the story that wants to be told through us. It is only by treating ourselves with love and kindness that we can reflect that experience on the page.

TODAY
Logging hours on the page need not be an exercise in masochism. If you are feeling despair, go outside and take a walk. A little distance from your story will make room for a wider perspective.

Until tomorrow,
Al

DAY 74

"Providence has its appointed hour for everything.
We cannot command results, we can only strive."
—MAHATMA GHANDI

STAYING OUT OF THE RESULT

"What is the market looking for?"

I hear this question from writers all the time, as if there's some secret they must figure out so that they can fulfill the marketplace's order. Like they're building widgets.

The truth is, we are the market: me and you, and everyone we pass on the street. If we were to ask people what they wanted to read, the majority of them would not say, "Vampire novels," or "Anything about wizards." People are not that specific with their tastes. Rather, what we are likely to hear is "I just want to read something good."

So, the question is "How do we write something good?" We do it by writing the novel that we've always wanted to write but are afraid to commit to paper. We do it by being willing to write the forbidden.

Could anyone have predicted that first-time novelist Kathryn Stockett's *The Help*, was going to sell millions of copies? What about Alice Sebold's *The Lovely Bones*, a novel about the aftermath of a young girl's rape and murder?

We must tell our story with all of the passion and honesty we can muster. When we write it for ourselves and let go of the idea that anyone else must read it, the market might very well beat a path to our door.

By giving ourselves permission to write what we are afraid to write, we will see our third act from a new perspective.

TODAY
1. Write for five minutes: "The one thing that I really want to say in this story, but am afraid to say is…"
2. Notice where this lives in your story.

Until tomorrow,
Al

DAY 75

"Great dancers are not great because of their technique, they are great because of their passion."

—Martha Graham

TECHNIQUE

Hi Writers,

Technique is developed over time. Through reading and writing we absorb a sense of story structure, of cadence and rhythm; we learn how to create and release tension. We deepen our relationship to the dilemma at the heart of our story. We grow in our understanding of human nature. Through sitting alone each day and allowing our imaginations to wander, and then writing down what we see, we develop what might be called technique.

Technique is a word often used by people who do not understand the process of creation. It can imply an outside-in approach, as if the artist simply harnessed his *technique* and voila, the work appeared. Technique involves cultivating a spirit of curiosity. Although there is a rigor to technique, it is really a marriage of intuition and many hours of practice.

I once had the opportunity to meet Paul Schrader, a hero of my youth. The brilliant screenwriter of the classic Martin Scorsese films *Taxi Driver* and *Raging Bull*, among others, had called me to discuss a story I had written. I mentioned how my third act had a problem in the hopes that he would offer a brilliant solution that would set me back on the path. He didn't. But what he said was even more helpful. "Kid, third acts are a bitch."

The relief I felt was indescribable. If my childhood hero struggles with third acts, maybe I can stop making meaning out of my own struggle. Just because writing is difficult, and sometimes near to impossible, does not mean we are not writers. Acknowledging the challenge often lessens the notion that we are supposed to figure it out. We must continue pounding away and trust that the story gods are guiding us.

TODAY

1. As your protagonist, write for five minutes, beginning with, "I will never be free until I..."
2. Where can you use this writing to clarify your protagonist in the story?

Until tomorrow,
Al

DAY 76

*"Whenever you find yourself on the side of the major-
ity, it is time to pause and reflect."*

—MARK TWAIN

THE ACT OF CREATION IS COUNTERINTUITIVE

Hi Writers,

When I was a teenager, I was an avid drummer. I had a great drum
teacher who taught me all sorts of rhythms. The bossa nova was a
bitch to learn, with the hands and feet seeming to work at cross-
purposes. It made my brain hurt but after many hours of practice it
became *second nature*.

In my early thirties I began painting and again, found a great
teacher who taught me about contrast, whether it was with color,
texture, or something I'd never heard of called *undercoating*. The
undercoat is the color underneath the image that provides depth
to the painting. For instance, if I'm painting a pale blue sky and a
dark barn, underneath the sky is a darker color like gray or brown,
while underneath the image of the barn is a light color, perhaps
cream or tan.

At first it was confusing to imagine the x-ray version before
painting the real thing. Plus, I am impatient. I wanted to get the
thing down on the canvas as fast as possible. But I discovered
quickly that without an undercoat the painting was lifeless. It had
no depth.

The process of writing a story involves a similar counterintuitive approach. If we were to just write our idea of the story, we would either get stuck halfway through, or at some point our story would begin to feel forced; it would lose its sense of having an organic throughline.

We began with an idea, or an image, or an impulse that is typically connected to some preexisting belief. This belief becomes the subtext that is explored through the events of the story (the plot). Through inquiring into the structure questions, the hero's want and need, and the dilemma, our relationship to the story grows beyond our idea of how it should go. It is not always comfortable. Images may emerge that seem at odds with our idea, but upon closer investigation we may discover that as our ideas shift, they also become clarified.

TODAY
In bullet points, quickly list the series of actions that the antagonists take in Act which lead to a new revelation for your protagonist.

Until tomorrow,
Al

DAY 77

*"Argument is to me the air I breathe. Given any prop-
osition, I cannot help believing the other side and
defending it."*   —GERTRUDE STEIN

STORY IS AN ARGUMENT

Hi Writers,

It is inevitable that we write about issues we feel strongly about.
Although we may not like to admit it, what we feel strongly about is
subjective, meaning it has an opposing argument. Our story begins
with a dramatic question, a hypothesis, and the plot is the argument
played out. It is through the plot that a deeper truth is revealed.
For instance, in *The Great Gatsby,* the plot's dramatic question is
"Will Gatsby win Daisy's love?" Gatsby loved Daisy years ago and
then he went off to war. In the meantime, she married Tom, who
is now having an affair. Although the plot explores the question of
whether or not Gatsby will succeed in his goal, the argument is really about whether or not it is possible to return to a more innocent
time. Through Fitzgerald's cast of characters, this question is visited
in every scene.

    Story is alchemical. It often involves two disparate elements col-
liding, thus leading to a new understanding. In *The Great Gatsby*, it
is the desire for love and the struggle to maintain one's social class.
It is the collision of these two elements that lead to the story's tragic

conclusion. In the rewrite it is helpful to revisit the dramatic question in order to explore dynamic ways to exploit the story.

If we find ourselves pushing an agenda, or trying to convince our reader to take a side, our story will lack true conflict. The argument will seem lopsided and the author's voice will begin to sound strident or manipulative. We must be willing to play the opposite side of the argument with equal integrity.

TODAY
1. What is the argument being played out through your plot?
2. What are the two disparate elements that collide in order to reveal a deeper truth?

Until tomorrow,
Al

WEEK TWELVE

THE BATTLE SCENE

This week we are rewriting up to the point where our protagonist makes a new choice. This is called the battle scene. Although it is an internal battle for the protagonist, it may manifest itself externally. It is where our protagonist makes a choice between what he wants and what he needs. It is a difficult choice and it is through this choice that the dilemma is resolved.

This scene likely already exists in our work. The challenge now is to make it as clear and specific as possible. It is not simply the choice that our hero makes that gives this moment its gravity, it is also the meaning ascribed to this moment.

QUESTIONS FOR THE WEEK:

1. What does my protagonist want?

2. What does my protagonist need?

3. Can I identify a scene in my work that shows the reader the difficult struggle between these two opposing forces?

4. How can I illustrate for my reader the struggle that this choice holds for my protagonist?

5. How is the dilemma resolved through my protagonist's choice?

6. Is the choice a surprise, while on another level, utterly inevitable?

DAY 78

*"All my life I always wanted to be somebody. Now I
see that I should have been more specific."*

—LILY TOMLIN

BEING SPECIFIC

Hi Writers,

It is easy to play it safe by intellectualizing this process. This is the quickest way to kill the aliveness in our third act. The human impulse is to avoid conflict, but as writers we must exploit the conflict and allow it to flourish.

Story is an emotional experience. If our reader is not emotionally involved, we are not doing our job. Are we being clear and direct? What are we trying to say? Have we said it, or are we dancing around it? Do we really understand it, or do we need to inquire further? There is often a tendency to vamp in the first draft. This is as it should be. We were searching for something, sometimes without even knowing what it was. We were chasing after the truth, trying to marry an impulse to an idea, trying to make order out of chaos, to capture a moment that causes our reader to wonder how the hell we knew that when she thought she was the only one.

But in the rewrite we comb through our work with a different agenda. We are searching for where we can tighten, layer, and dramatize exposition. How can we say something without spelling it out? How can we give our reader an *experience* rather than indicating what they should think or feel? Sentimentality is just an excuse for general writing. It leaves only the most distracted among us feeling satisfied and less alone. For everyone else, it does the opposite. Do not settle for platitudes. Our theme is only of value when it is thoroughly explored.

TODAY
1. List three pivotal scenes in your third act.
2. Taking two minutes on each one, quickly write down what each scene is about.
3. Allow this new clarity to inform your third act.

Until tomorrow,
Al

DAY 79

"Trust the instinct to the end, though you can render no reason."   —RALPH WALDO EMERSON

HALF-AWAKE STATE

Hi Writers,

When I wake up I often lie in bed and imagine my story from a half-awake state. When I am relaxed, my brain is unconcerned with logic. The inner critic is still asleep and I am open to nonlinear solutions. I imagine my characters and allow them to play out scenarios in ways I might not have considered. This can be a fertile time. With daylight comes the crashing reality of practical concerns, but if I can allow my imagination to wander first thing in the morning, it can provide me with ideas to explore in my morning writing session.

In rewriting Act Three, this exercise can be particularly helpful. We tend to hold onto our fixed ideas and this rigidity tends to grow as we have more at stake. By the time we get toward the end of our story we want to take over the reins, as if this job has now become too important to entrust to our channel. This type of thinking can be difficult to shake but if we can catch ourselves first thing in the morning, before we have time to latch too tightly to our preconceived notions, our imagination might surprise us with where it wants to go.

TODAY
Sleep in. In solving story problems, allow your imagination to play, unencumbered by your idea of how the problem *must* be solved.

Until tomorrow,
Al

DAY 80

"Cleverness is not wisdom."

—EURIPIDES

INNER WISDOM

Hi Writers,

The drive to create is evolutionary. Evolution is often thought of in physical or intellectual terms, whether it is growing lungs or developing the ability to reason. However, as artists we might also consider evolution in spiritual terms. As channels, we are inquiring into a place of fundamental knowing.

We do ourselves a favor in the rewrite when we allow our story to move in directions we had not expected in our first draft. It can be uncomfortable, even scary, as we may feel that we are derailing months of hard work, but our stories often subvert our own expectations. We can open up the opportunity for this to happen when he have a certain confidence in the basic direction of our story.

Each of us has innate wisdom that makes us uniquely qualified to write our story. Just as we are naturally drawn to exploring the nature of a dilemma, the resolution to the dilemma lies within us as well.

Do not confuse wisdom with morality or being "good." Wisdom is more basic than that. Wisdom is a way of seeing beyond the appearance of things to the way things actually are. Our inner wisdom is our connection to reality. How we respond to reality may inform our morality, but that response is different than wisdom.

It is also important not to confuse wisdom with having the answer. Getting more specific with our work is an ongoing process of shedding our idea of the story for the most dynamic version of the story. Just because the resolution lies within us does not mean that we necessarily have immediate access to it. It is a mysterious process, and through inquiry we are being led to the most dynamic version of our story.

TODAY
As you consider the ending to your story, notice that there is a sense of something that you know to be true. This knowing is not intellectual but springs from a deeper place and may even be contrary to what you believe to be true. Trust this knowing, as it is guiding you to the true ending of your story.

Until tomorrow,
Al

DAY 81

*"Dreams come true; without that possibility, nature
would not incite us to have them."*

—JOHN UPDIKE

WHAT IF?

Hi Writers,

If we are beginning to panic, overwhelmed by the sparse state of our
third act, we need to take a breath and relax. Everything we need to
know is within. The beginning of the writing process is exhilarating. We take off with energy and excitement, but at some point we
hit a wall. So much of this work happens in our subconscious, and
our job is to listen. Fear often arises when we realize that our idea of
our story will not get our hero to the end of the story. Sure, he's going to survive, but who cares? The hero's journey is a soul journey,
and the soul refuses to settle for mere survival.

We do this sometimes. We think, "God, just get me through
this day, this month, this life." Asking "What if?" can be frightening,
so we avoid it. The possibility of true freedom feels out of reach, so
we do not seek it. But asking *what if* is the stuff of great fiction. Asking *what if* is the stuff of Act Three. Act Three is about possibility.
What if we allowed our *idea* of our story to collapse? What if we
accepted that we just didn't know? Would we not be exactly where
our hero is? And how would that alter our perception?

A paradigm shift occurs in Act Three. It requires surrender. The hard part is trusting our hero's transformation even if we do not know how it is going to happen. We must bypass all of our conditioning, all of our cynicism, all of our ambition, to trust in that childlike place where we are moved by the truth of our story.

This is not weak sentimentality. I am not talking about Santa Claus and the Easter Bunny and tugging at the heartstrings. But I am talking about the struggle for love, which lies at the heart of every story, despite the tone, genre, and whether it is a happy ending or a tragedy. Love is the thing that is always on the table in every story.

We will know the ending is right because it will ring like a bell. We will have found some kind of order in the chaos.

TODAY
1. Write down what your hero wants.
2. Write down what your hero needs.
3. Notice how these two things are in conflict with each other.
4. Notice a scenario near the end of your book where she must make a choice between these two things.

Until tomorrow,
Al

DAY 82

*"We are so clothed in rationalization and dissem-
blance that we can recognize but dimly the deep primal impulses that motivate us."*

—JAMES RAMSEY ULLMAN

MAKING MOTIVES PRIMAL

Hi Writers,

Our characters are driven by primal desires. Anything less is un-
interesting and, frankly, untrue. A primal desire is not about big
emotions, it is about life-and-death stakes. Sometimes there can be
a temptation to bolster a character's motives by complicating his
reasons for the actions he takes. This usually has the opposite effect,
and can confuse the reader.

Let's say we are writing a story about a guy from Long Island
who robs a bank and decides to flee to Mexico to evade the authori-
ties. That is a primal motive – freedom. To give him a girlfriend
in Mexico might only confuse the reader. Is he going to Mexico
to evade capture or to be with his sweetheart? Better to give him
a fiancée in Long Island. In fact, perhaps the motive for his crime
was to pay for their wedding in the Hamptons and now he's torn
between love and freedom – two primal desires.

Everything in our story has been leading to the battle scene
where the dilemma is resolved, and the theme is made clear. When

we have more than one reason for a motive it might be a sign that we are not connected to our hero's primal drive, and without a clear primal drive, there will be no transformation.

This does not mean that our work is not nuanced, layered, complex and even ambiguous in its meaning, but all of this arises out of the character's primal desire to achieve a goal.

TODAY
Write down your protagonist's primal desire. Quickly track it through your story, noticing where it exists in each of the major story points. Are there any places in the story where the primal desire seems unclear? Can you make it clear?

Until tomorrow,
Al

DAY 83

"I went for years not finishing anything, because, of course, when you finish something, you will be judged . . . I had poems which were re-written so many times I suspect it was just a way of avoiding sending them out."   —ERICA JONG

PERFECTIONISM

Hi Writers,

Perfectionism has nothing to do with excellence. It is a desire to protect our ego. It can rob us of weeks, months, even years as we circle the same sentences and paragraphs, editing incessantly until, oftentimes, we return to the word or phrase we had originally chosen. We can waffle back and forth depending on our mood, in the hope that we will make our work unassailable.

Perfectionism is sneaky because it disguises itself as "hard work," but it is not. It is a way of hiding out. We have to be careful because if we allow it to run things, we may find ourselves not writing at all. We may become obsessed by our weaknesses, driven to think that engaging in any creative act is pointless when we will never be as good as our heroes who, we assume, never struggled with self-doubt but simply arrived fully formed on the published page.

It is difficult to argue with perfectionism. The good news is that we can use perfectionism against itself. Let's be curious about the *nature* of our perfectionism and consider how these impulses live in our characters. Perfectionism is universal and underneath it is fear. This fear manifests itself in different ways. When we explore the nature of our characters' obsessions, fears, and desire to control, we glimpse the true nature of perfectionism. Each one of us is an expert on perfectionism, and we can use this expertise to our benefit.

By exploring our perfectionism we can take the focus off the result and place it squarely on our story. In fact, our creative endeavor is an invitation to inquire into our *imperfections*. The opposite of perfectionism is not laziness or a lack of specificity, but rather humility. The belief that my work can be *better* is a fact, yet when we approach our work as if it is a math problem, it suffers. We destroy the aliveness of our story.

To some degree, we are always writing our story. There is a fine line between reading our story from the eyes of our *ideal reader* and reading it from some hypercritical perspective. We cannot please everyone. If we try, we will create nothing.

TODAY
Notice how your desire to control the outcome of your story offers clues into your protagonist's desire to control an outcome. Do you see a connection? Do you see how you are uniquely qualified to write your ending?

Until tomorrow,
Al

DAY 84

"If you can tell stories, create characters, devise incidents, and have sincerity and passion, it doesn't matter a damn how you write."

—SOMERSET MAUGHAM

TRUSTING THE SUBCONSCIOUS

Hi Writers,

There is a reason we wrote our first draft quickly. It was written from our subconscious, the seat of our genius. Our characters are archetypes, primal forces given voice to explore a dramatic question. The battle scene is where this question gets resolved and the story's theme is made clear.

We have all had the experience of being *in the zone*, of feeling as if the story was being told through us. However, the muse can be mercurial. Inspiration comes and goes. There may be moments of sweat and panic as we seek a coherent narrative. We may notice elements in our third act that now read as unrelated and ask ourselves, "Why was this written?" "What does this passage have to do with what I'm trying to say?"

Never delete something until you have explored why it *might* belong. Just because it seems out of place doesn't mean that our subconscious wasn't exploring something significant. Writing is humbling work. Our subconscious is not interested in protecting our ego. It wants the truth, which is often embarrassing and scary.

It is tempting to simplify these conflicts, to boil down a complex range of human emotions to the cold constraints of logic, but as we explore the battle scene, it is important to trust that what we wrote was written for a reason. Before we hit the backspace button, let us sit with our work long enough to gain clarity on *why* we wrote what we wrote.

This is challenging. It is difficult to sit in the place of not knowing, of looking at the material and thinking, "This is too complicated, I don't understand it." Our job is to remain curious about what these connections are. As we continue to investigate, we will be rewarded with insight that will shed light on the conflict and how it will be resolved.

TODAY
1. Write for five minutes, beginning with, "My story is about…"
2. Is your battle scene satisfying in a clear and specific way the points that you just outlined?

Until tomorrow,
Al

THE ENDING

OUR HERO RETURNS HOME

This week we are rewriting the ending to our story. The story does not conclude at the climax. It is not over until our hero is returned home. This final section is sometimes called the falling action or the denouement. It is not enough that our protagonist makes a new choice in the climax. Once the dilemma is resolved, we must see how this choice has altered her life.

It is also important to recognize that just because the dilemma is resolved, this does not mean that the there is no more tension. We want to see how the characters are relating differently as a result of the battle scene. All of our characters constellate around the dilemma. It is through seeing them at the end of the story that our theme is fully expressed.

QUESTIONS FOR THE WEEK:

1. How is my protagonist relating differently to other characters as a result of her journey?

2. What has she come to understand at the end that she didn't understand at the beginning?

3. Am I maintaining tension up until the final sentence?

4. What is the final image in my story?

5. Have I said everything that I set out to say?

6. Have I said it in the most compelling way?

DAY 85

"Everyone thinks of changing the world, but no one thinks of changing himself." —LEO TOLSTOY

RESOLVING THE DILEMMA

Hi Writers,

In attempting to keep the story interesting, there can be a tendency to veer away from the original idea. Sure, there is conflict, but it is not germane to the premise. For example: Years ago, I had an idea for a novel, a love story about two people who met approaching their middle years and were burdened by regret. They had made mistakes in their lives and were awash with guilt for the poor choices of their youth. She had married for status and not love and was now reeling from the crush of a loveless marriage. He had committed a terrible crime in a moment of drunken confusion and was recently paroled after serving twenty years in jail. As I wrote the story, I lost my way. On some level, I did not believe that it was possible to overcome regret. How does one forgive oneself for mistakes that cannot be undone? I could not *figure it out*. And so, instead, I wrote lengthy passages filled with weighty backstories and psychoanalytic profiles that would explain them. In short, I wrote around the central issue.

It was not until I got married that I recognized what I had been struggling with. My idea of overcoming regret still had condemnation in it. I had this idea that I needed to disprove the validity of their parent's choices in order to reframe their worldviews. In short, I was trying to win an argument. Yes, on some level story is an argument, but the argument is not won by being right but by being set free of the limiting belief that began the story.

I had been attempting to settle a score, which is another way of staying stuck. When I realized this, the story became simple. The dilemma that united the characters became quite apparent. The story was about intimacy. "If I expose my true self, will I still be accepted?" In fact, all of the characters in the story constellated around this dramatic question. The story became about the fear of risking one's true self, in spite of rejection, and ultimately it was about taking responsibility for one's choices.

TODAY
Giving ourselves what we need often involves a loss. What does it look like when your protagonist chooses what he needs? What must he let go? What is the cost? 5. How can you show this cost?

Until tomorrow,
Al

DAY 86

"The more one analyses people, the more all reasons for analysis disappear. Sooner or later one comes to that dreadful universal thing called human nature."
—OSCAR WILDE

FROM THE PERSONAL TO THE UNIVERSAL

Hi Writers,

There is a difference between reportage and storytelling. To report is to recount events, whereas storytelling provides a context for the events with the purpose of conveying a larger meaning. At times the difference can appear subtle. If we were just to read a few pages of a work, we might not notice a difference, but as we continue turning the page, we notice whether or not a story is building in meaning as it progresses.

Regardless of whether we are writing fiction or memoir, there must be a thematic consistency that connects our plot to our characters' driving wants. It is common, particularly for new writers, to assume that our reader understands our characters' motives, but unless we are showing them through action, it is quite possible that we are being unclear. Our prose may be well crafted; there may be tension and surprise, but if the characters' wants are not clearly defined in each scene, our reader will wonder what the story is about.

Our characters may have specific speech patterns and idiosyncrasies, and the world they inhabit may be filled with fascinating details, but we must not confuse detail with specificity. Simple amusements are not enough. Our story must be about something. Story explores a theme and our characters are a function of that theme.

I worked with a writer once whose memoir was a series of vignettes. Although the manuscript was well written, something was missing. The stories, as a whole, did not amount to much. It is not enough to say, "Well, this book is about my childhood." Certainly childhood is a universal experience, but unless the driving want is apparent, as well as the meaning ascribed to it, the scenes will lack narrative drive. As I continued to ask the writer questions, a pattern began to reveal itself and we discovered that his story was about the desire for security. The facts of his life were all being explored through the lens of this driving want. Once the driving want was apparent, he was able to revisit the vignettes and recognize where his protagonist's desire lay in each scene. By doing this, the work became more alive, and some scenes which had previously seemed random or unrelated became clear and provided meaning for the climax of the story.

I worked with another writer who had a somewhat glib writing style. Of course, there's nothing wrong with glibness, but when it is used as a defense or to disguise a lack of curiosity, it can lead to thematic vagueness. Sometimes, what we are writing feels a little close to the bone, and so we crack a joke. If our intention is simply to be funny without revealing character, we are not going to deepen our reader's relationship to the story. However, if the subtext of our character's glibness is revealed and our reader is made to understand why our character is behaving in such way, she will become invested in the story.

TODAY
1. Is your protagonist's driving want alive in the final pages of your manuscript?
2. How does this want look different than it did at the beginning of the story?

Until tomorrow,
Al

DAY 87

"He that wrestles with us strengthens our nerves and sharpens our skill. Our antagonist is our helper."
—EDMUND BURKE

WORTHY ANTAGONISTS

Hi Writers,

Sometimes we can be too easy on our hero and too hard on our antagonist. As we approach our ending, there can be a tendency to promote an agenda or to indicate the outcome, which is the surest way to kill the drama.

It is the writer's job to explore the antagonists' positions with equal integrity. We must be curious, rather than certain, of the outcome, even as we believe we know exactly how the story ought to end.

This is not to suggest that a character may not be as diabolical as we might imagine, but rather, that the reasons for their actions might be related to something that is all too human. The paradox in writing a dynamic ending is that in creating an ending to satisfy all that we set out to say, we may discover the true reasons for our characters' choices. These reasons may be surprising. It does not mean that our original idea of the ending is wrong, but rather that there are nuances we did not previously understand.

There are those overachieving writers among us who might

interpret this as a reason to never finish their work. We do not want to hold our story so loosely that we lose touch with the initial impulses that got us started.

This is the opposite side of the same coin. I have seen writers try to give birth to the same story over and over again. The rewrite process is about moving from the general to the specific. By staying connected to those impulses that got us started, we move toward a more specific relationship to our story.

TODAY
Are you being true to your antagonists in your ending? In earning his transformation, your protagonist often affects your antagonist in surprising ways. Write down three ways that your antagonists are relating differently to your protagonist in your ending.

Until tomorrow,
Al

DAY 88

"The most difficult part of painting is knowing when to stop."   —PABLO PICASSO

PREPARING TO RECEIVE NOTES

Hi Writers,

How do we know when we have finished our novel? The purpose of the rewrite is to fulfill two criteria.

1. Have we said all that we wanted to say?

2. Have we said it in the most compelling way possible?

Once we have satisfied these two criteria, we are ready for feedback. Very often our friends will have questions and may see things we did not. Perhaps there are areas that need clarification while other areas are so obvious that they are unnecessary.

We are going to get notes. We are going to get opinions. And we are going to remember the first thing we discussed in the rewrite. We do not abdicate authority over our work. Does this mean that people do not have helpful notes? Of course not. It just means that we cannot randomly take every note we are given without processing it through the filter of what we are trying to express.

Our story lives within us. Our challenge is to remain open to new ways of seeing our work while not losing touch with that ineffable impulse that got us writing in the first place.

TODAY
In five minutes write a sober assessment of your story as if
through the eyes of your ideal reader. We cannot please every-
body, but we can be honest about whether or not we have satisfied our objectives.

Until tomorrow,
Al

DAY 89

"Alchemy is the art of manipulating life, and con-
sciousness in matter, to help it evolve or to solve
problems of inner disharmonies."

—Jean Dubuis

STORY IS ALCHEMY

Hi Writers,

Story is alchemy. It is a marriage of two or more disparate elements that through the pressure of conflict lead to a deeper truth. For example, in *The Lovely Bones*, a young girl is raped and murdered. That is one element. The question of how her soul comes to rest is another element. Without either element, the premise vanishes. If it is a peaceful death there would be little drama, and if the afterlife question was not explored there would be nowhere for the story to go.

It is the convergence of these two elements that results in a dilemma for the hero. In the rewrite, we are seeking to winnow away what does not belong to clearly illustrate this struggle. At the heart of every story is love. Find the love. Find where it is sought, missing, misguided or misplaced, and there you will find the drama.

As we approach the ending of our story, our focus lies squarely on our protagonist's new understanding. As the dilemma is resolved, what does she now know to be true, and how is she relating differently to other characters in the story?

The theme is fully revealed at our book's close. Have we expressed what we set out to say? If we set out to write about unconditional love, did we end up writing about sacrifice? If we set out to write about forgiveness, did we end up writing about tolerance? If we set out to write about freedom, did our story end in a truce? Does our ending satisfy ourselves, or does it feel like a compromise? If we truly believe in our ending, we must fight for it.

TODAY
1. Have you illustrated your protagonist's shift in perception in all of its manifestations?
2. Make a list of any loose ends that still need to be tied up.

Until tomorrow,
Al

DAY 90

"The end of our exploring will be to arrive where we started and know the place for the first time."
—T.S. Eliot

WE ARE COMPLETING A CIRCLE

Hi Writers,

The paradox of a great ending is that it is a total surprise, and yet utterly inevitable. Stories are not simply about our protagonist arriving at a new destination; they are also about completing a circle.

In the end, our protagonist understands something that he did not understand at the beginning. Whether our story is a comedy or a tragedy, a transformation occurs. The world is seen through a new lens. Sometimes the characters' circumstances remain fundamentally unchanged, yet the world is understood in a new way.

It is helpful to revisit the beginning of our story in order to clarify our ending. Is there a chord that is struck in the beginning, an image or a recurring motif that can act as a bookend at the story's close? In *The Great Gatsby*, Jay Gatsby is first seen gazing eastward over his swimming pool toward East Egg where Daisy, the object of his desire, lives. And by the end of the story, Jay Gatsby lies dead in his swimming pool, from a gunshot wound. We are returned to this familiar landscape where we first met Gatsby, and now we see his world through a new lens. Fitzgerald could have had his character killed anywhere, but there is a reason that he chose to have him murdered at the house, and specifically in the pool. A swimming pool, particularly in the 1920s was a symbol of privilege and status. If a man of such wealth can be killed in his own home, while relaxing in his pool, are any of us safe? It is as if the author is saying that regardless of status, we can all fall victim to our nostalgic desires.

Our story reveals a transformation. Wisdom is earned, a basic truth is arrived at, and the dilemma is resolved. Everything that happens in our story, whether we are conscious of it or not, is in service to our ending.

TODAY

1. What is the final image in your story that completes your theme? Has everything in the story been leading to this moment?
2. Do you see a possible way to "bookend" this moment with your beginning?
3. Are there questions that remain to be answered in your final chapter?
4. Answer them.
5. Go celebrate.

Thanks for taking the trip.

Your fellow writer,
Al

i'm done. now what?

Congratulations on completing your book! Now let's talk about how to put it out into the world. Every writer dreams of the large advance that allows her to quit her day job, the glamorous book tour, and the adoring fans. While the publishing industry has changed dramatically in recent years, there will always be someone willing to pay top dollar to invest in the next big thing. But there is a difference between dreams and fantasies. If you are reading this chapter first, before doing the hard work of rewriting your novel, I can assure you there is nothing in what follows that will improve your odds of getting published. On the other hand, if you are a hardworking writer who strives for excellence, and whose sole goal is to build a body of work, what follows will prove helpful.

There is nothing practical about making the career choice to become a novelist. The risks are obvious. There is no author union, no health insurance, no guarantee of selling your work, and no job security. The profession has one of the highest rates of suicide, alcoholism, depression and divorce – and if you are looking to get rich, you are probably better off buying investment property. In fact, I read somewhere that a famous writer made more money selling his Manhattan duplex than he did in his entire writing career.

So, why do we write?

The irony is that if you talk to most successful novelists, they did not start writing to make money. They wrote because they had to. Yes, it is possible to auction your book to a major publisher, and if you can, you should. However, most careers are built slowly. There are steps involved. Here is a basic overview of some points to consider now that you have completed your book.

GETTING AN AGENT

The bottom line is that if you write for long enough, and produce enough material, and your writing is decent, eventually someone is going to want to sell your work. Literary agents are simply salespeople in the business of selling a product. Although they may appear to be mysterious entities behind cloud-kissing gates, they are just like us, except with sore eyes and constant paper cuts from reading loose manuscripts until the wee hours.

The best way to get an agent is through a referral. If you know someone who has an agent, ask them to read your work. If they like it, perhaps they will give it to their agent for consideration.

The second best way to get an agent is by submitting your work directly to them. Here is how the process works. Get a list of agents off the Internet. Just Google "literary agents" and you will find websites that have endless lists of agents. Another way is to look in the acknowledgement sections of books and find where they thanked their agent. If you are willing to part with twenty bucks for a month's access, I recommend that you sign up for www.publishersmarketplace.com. They have an enormous database of authors, agents and publishers. You can type in the names of authors you admire or who write in a similar genre as you, and the site will tell you who represents them.

Type an email that contains a brief bio of your writing career, followed by a brief description of your book, and then politely ask if the agent would be interested in reading your work.

Send this email to as many agents as you can. Most of them will not respond. Do not take it personally. They are busy, stressed-out people. Be polite. Be professional. If you want to shine, do so through the elegance of your prose. Do not be crazy. The publishing world is still situated primarily on the east coast, and they are frightened of crazy people. If you want to be crazy, move to California and become a television comedy writer.

Now, here's the difficult part.

Wait for a response. And while you are waiting, continue writing or you will go nuts. And continue sending out query letters to other agents.

There is a saying, "Polish it here and it shines over there." What this means is that if you continue to do everything you can do, eventually you are going to see results, and they may have nothing to do with all of the work that you did.

If you continue writing and continue sending out query letters, eventually you are going to get an agent because your next-door neighbor accidentally reads the manuscript that you threw into the garbage and she happens to have a brother-in-law who is best friends with J.K. Rowling's agent.

Polish it here. It shines over there.

That is how you get an agent.

GETTING PUBLISHED

Never send your work directly to a publisher. Virtually no publisher will read an unsolicited manuscript. It is not personal. They want to avoid liability issues. Pretty much the only way to get your work read by a publisher is through an agent. I know, I can hear your cries of frustration. "But how can I get published if I do not have an agent?!"

Here is what you can do: You can send your work to magazines and literary journals. Most journals accept unsolicited manuscripts. Be prepared for rejection. Again, it is not personal. Do not take rejection as a comment on the quality of your writing. There are a million reasons why journals do not accept stories. They might be looking for stories on horses that month, or they are burned out on drama and are looking for humorous pieces, or maybe the particular editor who read your work is in a foul mood and did not connect to your story.

Keep sending out your work. Every writer gets rejected. Eventually you are going to get published in a magazine, and the next time you send out a story or a section of your manuscript to an agent, you can proudly announce that you are a published author. Every small success builds on itself.

SHOULD I SELF-PUBLISH?

The stigma of self-publishing is gone. The physical quality of self-published books now rivals that of traditional publishers, while the content of self-published books is obviously far more erratic. The cost of self-publishing has made the process democratic and appealing to not only those who are unable to secure a traditional publisher, but to those who recognize that one is no longer a requirement to gaining and building a loyal readership.

The list of authors who have self-published their work through the years is impressive. Marcel Proust, Nathaniel Hawthorne, Virginia Woolf, Edgar Rice Burroughs, Jane Austen, Gertrude Stein, e.e. cummings, Henry David Thoreau, Emily Dickinson, and Dave Eggers, among countless others have all self-published their work at one point in their careers. If you are seeking a traditional publisher to validate your creative work, you are missing the point. A rejection from a traditional publisher is not necessarily a comment on the quality of your writing. It is simply a comment on how much money they believe they can make from selling it.

You will get to keep a larger percentage of the pie. You just have to decide whether the pie will be appreciably larger than with a traditional publisher and how much promotion you are willing to do.

Screenwriter William Goldman's famous line about Hollywood, "No one knows anything," is equally true in publishing. The decision of what to buy and what to pass on is as much a game of luck and timing as it is a measure of one's talent.

One of my former students wrote a book that was rejected by

dozens of agents and publishers. They all told her that the book was not commercial. Utterly frustrated, she decided to self-publish it. Six month later it was selling so well that a major publishing house offered her a six-figure advance for the rights.

Publishing companies are run by people. People are fallible. No one can predict with any certainty what will sell and what will sit on the shelves. No one knows anything.

BOOK PROMOTION

I used to believe that being a talented, diligent artist should somehow guarantee that one's work would find an audience. In fact, I used to look down on those creative types who were constantly self-promoting. It seemed cheap and brazen, and was clearly a sign that they were of inferior talent.

Writing and promotion are distinctly separate skills. I still don't love marketing, but I do genuinely like people and I am endlessly fascinated with the creative process, so talking about writing and the writing process is something that I enjoy.

I actually enjoy going on book tours, and even occasionally posting articles on Facebook. I used to think marketing was beneath me, but in fact, I was really just scared. The writing meant so much to me that I was afraid someone might not like it. Marketing is scary for artists because now we must publicly announce to the world that we would like them to buy someone that sprang from our imagination. To use an eighties term we have to *own our power*. On some level, we might even feel guilty for getting paid for doing something that does not feel like work.

Even if you are published by a traditional publisher – I have truly never heard of a single author who was satisfied with how their publisher promoted their book. This does not mean that the publishers do not do their best. It is just that there is only so much they can do. You are the channel for the work. You are the golden goose. The public wants to know you.

You may think that you would like to remain mysterious. That websites and social media and blogging are tacky. You are a serious writer and cannot be bothered wasting your time with such nonsense. I don't disagree with you. But I have never met a writer – and I know a lot of writers – no matter how high-minded their literary aspirations, who did not want a wider readership.

Yes, if a book is great, word of mouth will help it to spread. But not always. Until the book reaches a tipping point, it is out there competing for eyeballs with thousands of other books. And the amount of choices now is so mind-boggling that even if a book is terrific, it takes more than that to get people to read it.

WEBSITES

Every author should have a website. It should be clean and easily navigable. People want to know who you are, what you have done, how to contact you, what you are working on, how many pets you have, if you are married or single. They want to read articles on you. They want to know what you think about the world. Something strange happens when you are a published author. People feel like they know you. They have read your book. They have read your deepest thoughts. In a sense, they do know you. Your website is a way for your readers to connect to you. It should represent who you are. Many authors don't want to be bothered with this. It is understandable. You want to write. You don't want to concern yourself with thinking about and designing a website. If you are unconcerned with your book developing an ever-widening readership, you can skip this part. If the thrill of creation has satisfied you completely and all you want to do is write the next book, then by all means don't bother building a website. A website takes time and energy and it requires regular maintenance. But if you want people to know about your creative work, it is the cornerstone of your creative business.

SOCIAL MEDIA/BLOGGING

Are you on Facebook or Twitter? It is not enough to be on social media anymore. Our *books* need to be on it as well. Social media is the way we connect to our readers. There are an infinite number of creative ways to maintain this connection, from blogging about current events and social issues, to providing information and content, to holding contests and offering giveaways of products and services. I know some writers who hold regular competitions and offer their books as prizes. The competitions can be serious or silly, and can tie into themes in your book.

One of my students started blogging once a week about style and fashion and four years later, the material from her blog became a book. She had a built-in audience for the book, and when she self-published it, it became a hit. Six months later she sold the rights to a major house for six figures in a bidding war.

Make comments on other bloggers sites. Don't hype yourself, but mention who you are and what you do. Make sure that your comments are valuable. Blog posts cannot be infomercials. They must be content-rich. Talk about your experience writing the book. Talk about yourself. Find an angle and write about that. Because I am known as a writing teacher, I frequently write about the trials and tribulations of becoming a first-time novelist. I started a small publishing company called Writers Tribe Books, and one of my authors has started tweeting bon mots pulled from the narrator of his books.

The secret to social media is to be consistent. Don't binge and write six blogs in one day and then not write anything else for six months. In the beginning, there might be no one paying attention. That is okay. Just keep going. Write what interests you. Who knows? It may become your next book.

Do you have to write a blog to be a successful novelist? No. You don't have to do any of these things. I am pretty sure that Cormac McCarthy does not have a blog. But then again, it took him almost forty years of writing novels before anyone started reading him.

MEDIA/BOOK REVIEWS

There are many legitimate publications, such as *Kirkus Reviews, Publisher's Weekly* and *Library Journal* that review books. They typically take a few months to write a review and will only do so for books that are not yet available to the public. There is no guarantee that your book will get reviewed, but if you don't mind waiting a few extra months to find out all you need to do is send them an advanced reading copy of your book with a cover letter. Major publishing companies usually print up special copies of the book for reviewers. However, if you have self-published your book, you can simply put a sticker on the cover that states: Advanced Reading Copy.

You can also pay a periodical to print a review on your book. Of course, this does not guarantee that you will receive a positive review, but getting reviewed is one important tool in building awareness for your work. Prices vary widely based primarily on the scope of the publication's readership. Most reviews typically take from between six and eight weeks, but if you are willing to pay a premium, there is sometimes an express service. Below are some publications that offer reviews, along with some notes on what they charge.

1. Clarion
2. Kirkus Indie (sister company of Kirkus)
3. Book Pleasures
4. BookReview.com
5. ReaderViews.com

ARTICLES

You can write articles based on the topic that you have written about and link them to similar articles on the Internet.

BOOK READINGS

Once your book is available, schedule book readings. If your book is available through distributors such as Ingram, or Baker and Taylor, bookstores can order it directly from the warehouse. If your book is not available through a distributor, it is still possible to schedule a book reading. Bookstores are in the business of selling books. They are often willing to schedule an event if they think that can sell a lot of books. You can bring the books to the store yourself and sell them on consignment. The deal is typically 60% for the author and 40% for the store.

If you are going to call up a store and book an event, here is a basic rundown on how to approach it.

1. Be cheerful and upbeat. They don't know who you are, and they don't care that you are a genius. I cannot tell you how many book readings I have done where the staff has told me how refreshing it was to have someone so down to Earth. I never thought I was particularly down to Earth until I heard how some of these authors come in. Let's face it, public speaking can be terrifying, and sometimes there can be a tendency to compensate by adopting some weird, brooding persona. Just be yourself, unless you are a person who does not smile, in which case, try to approximate your regular persona, but with a smile.

2. Tell the manager that you have just published a book. Tell her the title, and that you are scheduling a book tour, and is she interested in having you read at her store. If she asks what the book is about, do not give her a ten-minute plot rundown or how the thematic elements of your crime novel were inspired by the early poems of Walt Whitman. It is not that she doesn't care, though she probably doesn't. She is incredibly busy. And if she is an indie bookstore, she is fighting to survive against the tide

of Internet commerce. Be nice to your indie bookstore personnel. They are modern-day saints.

3. Tell her that you are going to bring in lots of people. She is going to want to know how you are going to bring in people. And this is where you tell her that you have a website, and a Twitter account, and a monthly newsletter that goes out to thousands of people each month. Tell her that you are going to bring friends and family, and you are going to fill the place.

4. If you have convinced her that you can sell books, then she is going to want to know about the book. She might even ask you to send her a media kit. A media kit is simply a short explanation of the book, stating its target audience, and all of the things that you are going to do to make it a huge success.

AWARDS

There are hundreds of book awards. You can find them online and submit to them yourself. They generally require a small payment to cover administration costs, and usually four copies of the book in order to be considered. Winning awards is just one more way of gaining visibility and validating your work in the marketplace.

A FINAL THOUGHT

When someone says, "I want to be a writer," it does not make much sense to the ethos that forged this nation. America is a young country and not particularly given to introspection. This is why American writers, even successful ones, are often treated with disdain. If you do not believe this, go take a meeting in Hollywood.

The reason for this is that the writer has intrinsic power. The material originates with us. Without the writer, the publisher cannot publish, the agent cannot agent, and the producer cannot produce.

But the writer can still write.

And these days, he can even publish and produce his own work if he wishes. The writer's power is increasing daily. In Europe the artist has always been revered as a crucial and even sacred element of the culture. In America the writer's power is growing daily because she is no longer dependent on the previous infrastructure.

It is important to remember this. There can be a desperation on the part of the writer to acquire an agent, to get published, to get read, but we can forget the most important ingredient: the book.

All of our power lies in our ability to put our truth on the page.

Go to www.lawriterslab.com to sign up for my free monthly newsletter where you will receive information on free tele-course workshops as well as writing tips, author interviews, and lots more. I also promote alumni of the books and the workshops in the newsletter, so when your book is published, please let us know at info@lawriterslab.com and we will promote it for you. Just put ALUMNI NEWS in the subject heading.

STORY STRUCTURE QUESTIONS

By identifying the dilemma at the heart of our story, and noticing how it is alive in every scene, we are then able to inquire into the story structure questions. By exploring the questions that follow, we begin to see how our protagonist's dilemma never changes, and yet the manner in which he attempts to achieve his goal is constantly changing.

Though we often have a sense of where our story is not working, it can be helpful to understand why it isn't working. Through inquiring into the structure questions, we come up with solutions that provide our work with a thematic consistency that raises our story's stakes while building it in meaning.

These story structure questions are to be referred to in Week One as we create a new outline. The questions are written in order and are the key story points in our hero's journey. In the first draft, we inquired repeatedly into these questions, and simply wrote down whatever images appeared.

As we do a new outline prior to our rewrite, we might consider proportioning our Acts to be roughly as follows: Act One is about one quarter of the length of your story, while Act Two is two quarters, and Act Three is one quarter. As always, there are no rules, but if we find that our first act runs two hundred pages, and the entire book is only three-hundred pages, then there may be a problem with the story's structure. It is also common to discover that the story points are not what we thought they were. We may have had an idea of where our first act ended, only to discover that it ends somewhere else, or that scenes from our first act belong later in the story. By inquiring into the structure questions we can get an overview of our story and have a basic confidence in the way it will be told before diving into the specifics. In this way, less time is wasted in rewriting scenes that may never make it to the final draft.

ACT ONE

- OPENING/FALSE BELIEF: How does my story begin? What is my protagonist's false belief that gets reframed at the end of the story?

- DILEMMA: What is my protagonist's dilemma, and how can I describe it in universal terms?

- INCITING INCIDENT: What event happens that causes my protagonist to respond?

- OPPOSING ARGUMENT: How does an antagonist respond to the protagonist, thus illustrating the nature of the protagonist's dilemma?

- DECISION: What decision does my hero make that he can't go back on, and what is the reluctance that precedes this decision?

ACT TWO

- BEGINNING OF ACT TWO: How has my hero's decision altered his world? What is he struggling with now that he was not struggling with in Act One?

- FALSE HOPE: What is the first sign of growth or success that my hero experiences toward achieving his goal? How does this moment illustrate the protagonist's idea of what his goal should look like?

- MIDPOINT: How is my hero tempted in the middle of the story between what he wants and what he needs? This is the point in the story where he could go back to where he was or plunge into the unknown and risk losing everything. What does his choice look like at this point in the story?

- SECOND HALF OF ACT TWO: How has my hero's new choice altered his relationship with his antagonist, and thus raised the stakes?

- SUFFERING: What does it look like when my hero realizes that this is more difficult than he had imagined? How does he suffer?

- SURRENDER: What would it look like if my hero realized that what he was pursuing was impossible to achieve? How does he reframe his relationship to his goal?

ACT THREE

- HERO ACCEPTS THE REALITY OF HIS SITUATION: What is my hero's reality that he is beginning to accept, and what action does he take as a result?

- ACTION: My hero takes action toward giving himself what he needs.

- BATTLE SCENE: What event happens that forces my hero to choose between what he wants and what he needs? How does this choice resolve his dilemma?

- HERO RETURNS HOME: How does my hero's choice return him to a new equilibrium, where he understands something about himself and his world that he did not understand at the beginning of the story?

ACKNOWLEDGEMENTS

Thank you to Amy Inouye for book production – you are a joy to work with. Thanks to Ryan Basile for doing the cover design – you are a kind and patient man, as well as a true artist. Thanks to Lisa Hanson, Mindi White, Ashley Jean Granillo, Alissa Binder and Rebecca Johnson for proofreading and copy-editing – I am so grateful for your notes. Thank you to my passionate staff at L.A. Writers' Lab – truly you are the smartest and wisest writing teachers in the business, and I am so lucky to have you working at the lab. A special thank you to all of the writers who have ever picked up one of these books, or passed through the doors of one of our classes, or graced the phone-lines of one of our tele-course workshops – this book could not have been written without your ongoing curiosity, insight and feedback. These pages will always necessarily be a work in progress. As your fellow writer I am honored and privileged by your trust and support. Finally, thank you to my wife, Mary-Beth, my lucky charm, my inspiration, and the one whom I can't wait to see when the writing is done.

TODAY'S ORIGINAL VOICES

Death by Sunshine by Allison Burnett
B.K. Troop is an aging, erudite, chemically imbalanced, gay, alcoholic novelist living in Manhattan. His life is turned upside down when he is invited to Los Angeles to adapt one of his novels into a screenplay. Soon after his arrival, B.K. is thrust into the heart of a mystery that only he can solve. With the help of his trusty Mexican chauffeur, B.K. penetrates the lower depths of Hollywood with hilarious and surprisingly poignant results.

Raymond Carver Will Not Raise Our Children by Dave Newman
Dan Charles is a writing professor living on the outskirts of Pittsburgh with his wife and their two children. He is struggling to survive and to write books. This hilarious and heart-breaking tale tells the real story of what it means to be a writer of fiction in America.

Days Are Gone by Alan Watt
Alice has just walked out on her aging rock star husband. In her drive up the coast to visit her family, her life changes forever. Stuck in a small Oregon town, a relationship develops between herself and Webb Cooley, a recently paroled convict. In their attempts to lose themselves in each other, they are forced to confront their pasts and to move on with their lives.

East Bay Grease by Eric Miles Williamson
This blue-collar coming-of-age story set in Oakland, CA. was first published in 1999 and has become a modern classic. It has been published and distributed in over a hundred countries on every continent except Antarctica. France's leading literary magazine *Transfuge* named Williamson one of the "douze grands ecrivains du monde," twelve great authors of the world. *The New York Times Book Review* calls Williamson's prose "transcendent."

BOOKS ON WRITING

AVAILABLE NOW

AVAILABLE IN 2013

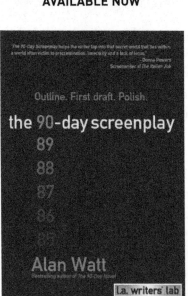

AVAILABLE IN 2013

AVAILABLE IN 2013
[All profits donated to PEN Center USA]

CPSIA information can be obtained
at www.ICGtesting.com
Printed in the USA
BVOW06s2156281017
498930BV00008B/101/P